Hartmann 11/91 & 7. 1

Into the Mouths
of Babes

Into the Mouths of Babes

A Natural Foods Cookbook for Infants & Toddlers

Susan Tate Firkaly

BETTERWAY PUBLICATIONS, INC.
WHITE HALL, VIRGINIA

Published by Betterway Publications, Inc.
White Hall, VA 22987

Cover photograph by Sam Abell
Illustrations by Marion Reynolds, © 1984
Typography by East Coast Typography, Inc.

Library of Congress Cataloging in Publication Data

Firkaly, Susan Tate
  Into the mouths of babes.

  Bibliography: p.
  Includes index.
  1. Cookery (Baby foods)   2. Cookery (Natural foods)
3. Infants — Nutrition.   I. Title.
TX740.F53   1984   641.5′622   84-14620
ISBN 0-932620-35-3 (pbk.)

Printed in the United States of America
098765

Dedicated to Zachary and Molly
my official taste-testers, mess-makers, and joy givers!

Acknowledgments

Without the support and encouragement of so many friends and family members, this book would not have been completed. A very special thank you:

to Laurel Sovich Schultz, Sarah Ackerman, Brent and Carol Jenkins, Denise Abell, Carol Langer, Alice Gerow, David Slezak, Newman Campbell, Molly, Laura and Bill Newman, Larry Lawwill, Dr. Bruce Campbell and Paula Campbell, Ron and Cheryl Lewis (and especially to Cheryl for taking the photo for the back cover)

to my support group — because they did — and to friends too numerous to list who always asked "How is your cookbook coming?"

to my parents, Helen and Ray Tate, for respecting my decisions in feeding our children

to Dr. Ray Wunderlich for his Foreword and his time and comments in the early stages of this manuscript

to Dr. Bill Ober and Maggie Ober for their comments, corrections, and encouragement

to Deanna Hammond, Pam Johnson, and Laura Michael for their typing and word processing assistance. And to Therese Titus and Joseph Harding for their editing.

to Robin Toth for use of several recipes from *Naturally it's Good . . . I cooked it myself!*

to Jackie and Bob Hostage for giving me the chance to share this book with others

to Molly and Zachary — without them I wouldn't be a mother and because of them I have learned so much

to Michael — for always being there.

Contents

Foreword by Dr. Ray Wunderlich, Jr. 11

Introduction 15

1. Why Make Your Own Baby Food? 19
2. Your Kitchen Layette 21
3. A Shopper's Guide to Whole Foods 25
4. Into the Mouths of Future Moms 35
5. Infant Nutrition 39
6. Feeding Your Baby 55
7. Coping with Food Allergies 67
8. Beginner Recipes 77
9. Intermediate Recipes 83
10. Advanced Recipes 89
11. Toddle Food Recipes 105
12. Whole Family Recipes 119
13. Recipes for the Allergic Child 145
14. What *Not* to Put into the Mouths of Babes ... 155

Bibliography 159

Index 163

Foreword

by Dr. Ray Wunderlich, Jr.

The amazing productivity and technology of modern-day America sees to it that American babies rarely, if ever, go hungry. A ready supply of commercial baby food provides sustenance for babies at any hour of the day.

The quality of commercial infant foods took a giant step forward when manufacturers, responding to public demand, produced foods free of sugar and salt. Nevertheless, baby food in a jar is "overcooked" (12 times) to kill bacteria and spores (e.g. botulism). Thus, babies who consume food exclusively or predominantly from commercial sources are ingesting food that is relatively old, and far from fresh. Furthermore, roach droppings have been found underneath the lids of baby food jars.

A growing number of concerned professionals and parents questions the quality of foods that, of necessity, must be "cooked to death" in order to be safe for human consumption.

There is no question that commercial, jarred baby foods fit readily into the convenience lifestyle of many American families. The tragedy is that too many families rely upon such food rather than utilizing it for those occasions (travel, for example) when home food preparation may be difficult. We pay a price for convenience. That price, as far as nutrition is concerned, is poor health. Degenerative disease in adults has its roots in childhood. Decades of wrong eating habits incubate and combine with other factors to produce catastrophic and chronic disease.

Irrespective of major societal change, the institution of family has not yet been supplanted as the prime shaper of responsible human citizens. In a family, kitchen arts are part and parcel of successful living. Choice of food, preparation of meals, and lively social intercourse at mealtimes are crucial components of family values. Good advice is to put your kitchen back a hundred years. A man or woman can claim the market, the kitchen, or the feeding role as his or her domains. Children *must not* be allowed to adopt eating styles by default. The best nutrition teacher is a family model that routinely consumes fresh, whole foods.

The author wisely counsels that the parent must feel comfortable in the role of dietician for the child, even though perfection, as far as desirable foods, may not exist.

The reader should be cautioned that the steady, monotonous use of any one food for baby is usually undesirable. A wide variation in foods provides greater nutrient exposures than does narrow food selection. In addition, rotating foods in the diet prevents some food allergies or allergy-like reactions to foods. In the case of peanuts and peanut butter it is especially important to avoid monotonous regular use. Peanuts have been found to induce atherosclerosis. One may also become allergic and/or addicted to them. Finally, a diet that relies extensively on one food such as peanuts excludes (displaces) other foods that also have nutrient value. Many persons wisely choose to limit peanut butter to occasional use and to more regularly use sesame, cashew, or almond butter.

The author rightly emphasizes the importance of high-nutrient foods before the birth of the child as well as after the child is born. Bravo for the message that good food along with love are the most vital ingredients for child health and prosperity!

Advice to commence infant feedings with cereal grains may be all right for some, but the use of vegetables as first food must be mentioned as a possible advantage.

Perhaps the most compelling advice in this book is the author's admonition to see to it that babies have successes and failures through trying. "They'll never learn to eat until we let them try, slop, and spill."

The "early" introduction of cottage cheese and yogurt at 4 to 6 months of age could be a sensitizing factor for many children. Many infants fail to mount an identifiable allergic reaction to milk products only to emerge later in life with various health problems associated with milk allergy. The intermittent use of cow-milk products probably is safer.

Susan Firkaly's genius is to transmit to the reader, simply and directly, her quiet, confident philosophy. She revels in child rearing using feeding as a positive expression of her care, concern, and direction. She wisely states, when one is on the receiving end of derisive comments or criticism from others, "let them go over your head."

Reading this book leaves one with a good feeling. When one follows the wholesome suggestions contained within it, the reader will have many good feelings as well as the benefit of improved biological health.

The frontline against disease is optimal diet. The sooner one implements a diet for health, the greater the dividends. *Into the Mouths of Babes* provides practical know-how for parents and children to live in a convenience-oriented society and yet to have the nutrients needed for sound mental and physical health.

Ray C. Wunderlich, Jr., M.D.
Preventive Medicine and Health Promotion
St. Petersburg, Florida

Introduction

Somewhere around the middle of my first pregnancy, it occurred to me that I soon would have the task of deciding what to feed our baby. When to give vegetables? How soon to give whole milk? How much milk should be given? How often? While studying everything I could on the topics of pregnancy and childbirth, I also began the search for answers to my questions and the study of infant nutrition.

Over the past eight years, I have pored over pages of information and ideas on infant feeding and found amazing contradictions in numerous areas. Where conflicting informed opinions existed between starting ages for a certain food, I usually chose the later starting date. Children have their entire lives to eat a variety of foods. I saw no reason to rush the introduction of too many foods too early and thereby risk possible allergic reactions.

The purpose of this book is to provide a variety of whole food recipes you can use instead of or along with prepared baby food. Although there is no single right way to feed your baby, *Into the Mouths of Babes* can be used as a guide to infant feeding, along with your instincts and your pediatrician's advice. (After all, there were mothers and fathers before there were pediatricians!)

Both mothers and fathers can easily follow these recipes. Most books assume the mother prepares food for "her" baby. Today, many more fathers take an active role in all aspects of parenting. Sex-biased and stereotyped books on child-rearing and feeding are unfair to the many men at home with their children, or those fathers sharing child-rearing responsibilities. With this in mind, I often use the word "parent" or "grown-up" instead of "mother".

The recipes in this book contain no meat. Since the birth of our first child, Zachary, eight years ago, our family gradually has developed a change in eating habits, from the typical meat and potato menu to a more natural foods and meatless diet. The expense of meat alone has caused many of us to look for cost-saving but nutritious alternatives. We began by including a meatless meal every other night in menu planning.

As we gradually moved to a vegetarian diet, (we eat meat occasionally and we do include chicken and fish in our diet) we found we felt better after eating. Our digestive systems didn't need to work as hard to digest and eliminate plant and vegetable protein, and we actually felt more energetic after meals instead of overfed and ready for a nap. We liked not eating as much of chemically fattened animals. For Zachary, meat was even more difficult for his infant body to digest.

Many parents will choose to wait until after the first year to introduce meat. Some might choose a regular meat diet while others will choose to raise their child on a vegetarian diet. These recipes can be helpful regardless of choice. It is important to be comfortable with your choice and knowledgeable about whatever eating plan you may choose.

Realizing the need to provide ample protein in our meatless diets caused us to learn more about other foods or food combinations high in protein. From reading Frances Moore Lappé's book, *Diet for a Small Planet,* I gained valuable knowledge about protein complementarity (the proper combination of plant proteins or non-meat animal protein to achieve a quality protein equal to or better than meat sources). I then developed new recipes for our family by using such food combinations as rice and beans, wheat and milk, or beans and cheese. It was a challenge at first but soon became routine. Feeling good about Zachary's diet, I began to collect the recipes I used for his meals. When Molly was born four years later, I devised even more recipes and concoctions for her. As my recipes grew and my scraps of paper overflowed my recipe box, I realized others might like to try these recipes for their babies, too. After laboring for several years, I finally was able to give birth to *Into the Mouths of Babes.*

Many parents prefer just opening a jar and feeding their babies with only seconds of preparation. Can they be blamed, with only 24 hours in a day and a baby taking up 23 hours? Presented here are nutritious recipes that are nearly as quick and easy to prepare as store-bought products. There are also recipes for preparing large batches to be frozen for later use.

Whether working inside or outside the home, we all need time-saving ideas so we're not chained to the high chair.

The recipes are divided into 6 sections: *Beginners* (for ages 4-6 months), *Intermediates* (for ages 7-9 months), *Advanced* (ages 10-12 months), *Toddle Food* (ages 1 to 2), and then a *Family Foods* chapter (providing a variety of wholesome recipes for all ages so that a natural progression from infancy can be continued.) Also included is a section *Recipes for the Allergic Child.*

Preparation time varies but many of the recipes can be prepared in ten minutes or less. The recipes that take a little longer to prepare can be planned easily around your family's meal for that day. Although I love to cook I always have found menu-planning an unlikable chore. I also found it's worth taking 10-15 minutes to plan a weekly menu rather than sighing and groaning around the kitchen just prior to mealtime. Having family members call out their suggestions to you when planning can be quite a help and also lets everyone share in the "fun" of menu-planning.

Before the recipe section you will find information on the hows, whats, and whys of feeding your baby. This book also includes basic information needed to understand infant nutrition. The infant nutrition chapter follows a section about pre-natal nutrition, *Into the Mouths of Future Moms.*

Along with information for infant and prenatal nutrition there also are three important food charts to help in your menu-planning: The Basic Four, The Meatless Basic Four, and the Allergic Basic Four.

Because of increased awareness and diagnosis of food allergies, I have included a chapter entitled *Coping with Food Allergies.* It provides background information and recipes that can help parents and children in dealing with food substances that often cause harmful reactions.

I have written this book so I could share recipes with others concerned about foods their children eat. With the exception of the recipes in the allergy section, each recipe has been taste-tested by our children, Zachary and Molly, and has met with their approval.

Good nutrition can be a lifelong gift to our children. As parents we have the responsibility to provide nourishment that will help our beautiful little people blossom into beautiful, healthy big people. The recipes and ideas contained in this book will help in providing your child with the best start possible for a healthful journey through life.

1 Why Make Your Own Baby Food?

In this high-tech age of microwave ovens and ready-prepared foods, why bother making your own baby food? It is so easy to open a jar . . . but, the comparison between what is in that jar and what is in home-prepared "Baby's Own" is quite noteworthy.

The nutritional superiority of a homemade product probably is the best reason to make your own. The concerned parent who elects to make baby food from scratch can choose fresh vegetables, fruits, and grains to serve without adding any unnecessary ingredients. Homemade products don't need preservatives to lengthen shelf life, because they are used fresh daily or quickly frozen for later use.

It's more economical! When making ones' own baby food, there is no expense for the jars, labor, bright packaging, advertising, or "extra" ingredients. The cost of a baby food jar alone often comprises one-third of the cost passed on to the consumer. Many commercial jars of food contain water — the consumer pays for that liquid weight. Of course, homemade brands contain water, but it's *your* water, prepared with *your* fresh ingredients.

We often can come up with foods for our baby from the grocer's "adult food" shelves, not only from the baby food aisle. Buying "regular" natural juices instead of baby juice will save on the grocery bill. Those juices can be diluted a bit at home (or strained in the case of orange juice) and given to your baby.

Many commercially prepared baby foods contain "modified starch" to keep the food from separating and to act as a thickening agent. This starch is treated with acids in the process of being made into this unnecessary thickening additive.

Many commercially prepared baby foods still contain salt and sugar. The nutrition awareness of consumers, however, recently forced companies to remove these unnecessary ingredients from most of their baby foods.

There is one ingredient that neither Gerber nor Heinz adds — and that ingredient is your LOVE. Preparing and sharing food, especially with your own family, feels good, and being able to add that loving touch feels even better. The self-satisfaction of knowing the food you make contains only the best ingredients is yet another reason to make your own.

Some recipes require some time to prepare. It would be wise to prepare them when spare time allows so that, on a daily basis, less preparation would be needed. As an example, oats can be ground in a food processor or blender, placed in a clean jar, labeled, and then used daily as needed. Batches of vegetables can be made up all at one time, frozen in ice cube trays (see *Your Kitchen Layette* chapter) and used later. Most other recipes take 10-15 minutes or less to put together. The time, energy, and caring it takes to prepare these foods can be considered a daily gift of good nutrition to your child.

Giving your child nutritious foods that are served in a loving, peaceful manner is much more important than knocking yourself out by trying to make every single food that enters your baby's mouth. It's so important to feel comfortable in your role as "dietitian" for your child. Some people might be happy making fruits and vegetables but buying prepared cereals rather than grinding and cooking their own grains. That's great! Some people might buy some foods and make homemade foods when they have time. That's great too! There is no single absolutely right way of feeding your baby. One might choose to buy some of the baby foods (cereals, for instance), and make others at home, or perhaps decide to make everything from scratch. Whichever you opt for — have fun!

2 Your Kitchen Layette

Clean hands, utensils, and cookware in the kitchen are vital for the preparation of safe, homemade baby food. Take inventory of the cookware you already have, and then add any of the following items that will help to complete your "kitchen layette".

(It is not necessary to have *all* of these items in order to make your baby's food — just as it is not imperative that a baby have six side-snap undershirts, five kimonos, six sleepers, six pairs plastic pants, etc.! After you read through some recipes, your own judgment can be a good guide.)

TO PREPARE: Baby food grinder   Food mill
Blender   Food processor
Grater   Pressure cooker
Steam Basket

TO STORE: Ice cube trays
Plastic freezer or bottle bags
Glass jars

TO SERVE: Bib
Baby spoon
High chair
Spouted cup
Heated baby dish

TO TRAVEL: Lunch box
Thermos

BABY FOOD GRINDER — a vital necessity! Ask anyone who has ever used one — they're great! For at home use, just put the foods you want puréed into the cylinder, grind, and serve right from the grinder. Whip it out at a restaurant or at a friend's house for dinner, and add the foods you select for your baby. It is like carrying a miniature blender in your purse or diaper bag. These cost about $5.00, and are worth every penny!

BLENDER — a great time saving appliance if you seriously plan to prepare your baby's food. It doesn't have to have 18 speeds — any old blender that "blends" will do!

GRATER — a small hand grater is needed for some of the vegetable recipes. A food processor would be a real treat to have, but a grater works "great."

STEAM BASKET — a collapsible steam basket is needed for cooking vegetables with steam. This inexpensive basket fits inside a saucepan containing about one inch of water. (Water should not touch the vegetables.) After covering the saucepan with a tight-fitting lid, steaming vegetables over medium heat is an easy way to cook — there is no need to stir. Steaming (but not overcooking) is a good way to save the valuable vitamin content in vegetables.

FOOD MILL — these are larger versions of the baby food grinder, allowing larger amounts of foods to be blended at one time. While not a necessity, a food mill can be useful in preparing baby food, particularly if a blender or food processor is not already in your kitchen.

FOOD PROCESSOR — if interested in saving time in the kitchen, this appliance will be a delight. It blends, purées, grates, or grinds a larger amount than the blender. A food processor is not necessary for baby food making, but it can help save time in many ways.

PRESSURE COOKER — this time-saving, nutrient-saving device is wonderful for cooking large batches of fruits, vegetables, and other foods. Although a pressure cooker is not essential to prepare these foods, it is a big help. Many people fear these because they've heard horror stories about the lids flying off and green beans all over the ceiling. A pressure cooker need not be feared if: (1) you read and follow the directions; and (2) you don't leave the pressure cooker on while you go out shopping.

People who use their pressure cookers love them. So dig out that *Presto* you got for a wedding gift, read the directions, and pride yourself on finding another way to save time away from the kitchen.

ICE CUBE TRAYS — a few ice cube trays are needed for freezing large quantities of fruits and vegetables. As soon as the cubes are frozen, plop into a plastic bag, label, date, and keep in freezer.

PLASTIC FREEZER BAGS — these can be used to hold the various frozen food cubes prepared in your kitchen. They are clean and designed for freezer use. Be sure to label each bag. It's amazing how things can get lost in a freezer! The individual, sterile plastic baby bottle bags are wonderful for traveling — whether out to a friend's for lunch or a 5 hour trip to see the grandparents.

Place several cubes in the bag, close tightly with a twist-tie, and serve your baby the thawed out food at mealtime.

GLASS JARS — sterile glass jars (canning jars or peanut butter jars) are good for storing ground oats or other grains. Remember to label each jar, or you will be amazed at how everything looks the same next time you check your shelf!

BIB — unless you're a masochist — a few bibs on hand go a long way in saving a parent's sanity. They eliminate (almost) food stains (watch out for peaches and bananas) and keep your baby from getting sticky and gooey (at least where the bib is).

BABY SPOON — a slender spoon made just for baby's mouth must be much easier on him than an adult-size spoon. (Imagine eating your cereal from a serving spoon — good tasting, but mouth stretching!) Some babies seem to prefer the plastic-coated spoons; others are just glad they are fed!

HIGH CHAIR — a high chair is a wonderful invention. It provides baby with a comfortable place to eat and grown ups with a little bit of breathing time. Be sure baby is secured safely in the seat belt but never assume your baby won't slip out or stand up and fall out of the chair. The tray provides a nice place for finger foods that baby can reach for or push all over the floor! An old plastic tablecloth placed beneath the high chair is a wonderful floor or carpet saver.

SPOUTED CUP — a small size cup with lid and spout top is great for introducing the cup to your six-month old baby. By 8-9 months, the idea of a cup will be second nature. Encourage your baby to hold the cup. Many children are weaned from breast milk at 12 months, and go successfully to the cup. Avoid buying the weighted "No-tip" cups. They're often too heavy for a baby to pick up successfully.

HEATED BABY DISH — this is helpful and convenient, but not a necessity. They are great for melting your frozen food cubes, but a small saucepan (egg poaching size) will do the job fine. Any small bowl can be used to serve the food.

LUNCH BOX — a lunch box to carry little food cubes, pieces of cheese, or a thermos of juice when going out for the afternoon or evening is really useful. Plastic, metal, or thermal lined all work well. Remember to include a bib, spoon, baby cup, and wet washcloth in a plastic bag for quick face and hand cleaning. A wet washcloth in a plastic bag added to a purse, diaper bag, or lunch box saves money on baby wipes, and often comes in handy.

THERMOS — inside every lunch box can be a thermos carrying baby's juices. Many restaurants do not have a good juice selection so having a thermos handy will guarantee your child of a nutritious drink.

3 A Shopper's Guide to Whole Foods

A natural foods diet for baby should contain a variety of wholesome foods. This chapter contains a guide to whole foods that can be substituted for processed, bleached, refined, or artificial foods.

Eight years ago none of the "strange" foods listed below were in our kitchen cupboards. Today these items are often on our grocery list.

Yogurt	Avocado
Tofu	Whole-wheat Flour
Millet	Barley
Dry Milk	Soy Beans
Garbanzo Beans	Lentils
Spinach	Sprouts
Honey	Bulghur
Sesame Seeds	Rice Cakes
Granola	Pita Bread

The chart on the next page offers some suggestions for substitutions you can make that will provide your family with a more nutritious, wholesome diet. If you have eaten very few of these foods and at first glance find many of the baby food recipes "strange," you are not alone! If you want to feed your child natural foods and are attempting to change your own diet, try adding these foods to your daily menu slowly. Trying one or two new foods a week will help you more than sitting down to a dinner of bulghur, sesame seeds, tofu, and sprouts!

Better Nutrition Substitutions

INSTEAD OF	SUBSTITUTE
artificial colors, flavors	natural colors and flavors
canned vegetables	fresh vegetables
chocolate	carob
colored cheeses	white, natural cheeses
cornstarch	arrowroot
double acting baking powder	single acting baking powder
hydrogenated peanut butter	fresh, natural peanut butter
mayonnaise	safflower mayonnaise, home-made mayonnaise
meat	non-meat protein combinations
prepared packaged cereals	natural cereals, your own cooked grain cereals
refined oil	safflower, peanut, corn, soybean, or sunflower oil
vanilla flavoring	vanilla extract
salt	sea salt
sugar	honey, molasses
white cornmeal	yellow cornmeal
white flour	whole wheat flour
white rice	brown rice

NATURAL COLORS AND FLAVORING

Read the label to find out if these are natural or synthetic. Unfortunately, most prepared foods found at the supermarket contain some kind of synthetic additives. Artificial colors and flavorings are now known to be contributing causes of hyperactivity and learning disabilities in children. Many adults have allergic reactions when they eat foods containing chemical additives. Natural additives include: colorings from vegetable juices, herbs, spices, salt, fresh fruit acids, brewer's yeast, and wheat germ.

FRESH VEGETABLES

Fresh vegetables surpass canned vegetables in flavor and nutrition. Using the pressure cooker will save time and nutrients. Shop for fresh, undamaged vegetables.

CAROB

Carob is made from ground pods of the honey locust tree. Although it looks like chocolate, it does not contain caffeine, sugar, vanillin, or emulsifiers. Babies who never have tasted chocolate (and they should not anyway before the age of three) find a carob drink quite a treat. For us chocolate lovers, it takes experimenting with carob for a while to discover it can be quite likable!

Carob powder (sometimes called flour) is low in fat and offers valuable minerals, unlike its chocolate "cousin". Carob is a bit sweeter than cocoa so you need to reduce the amount of sweetener if substituting carob powder in some of your favorite chocolate recipes.

NATURAL CHEESE

Processed cheeses usually can be spotted quickly by their orange or yellow color. Good old American cheese is made from natural cheeses, but before it is packaged — it is ground, blended, emulsified, heated, artificially colored, mixed with water or milk solids — and sometimes preservatives — then pressed into a smooth plastic-like mass. Natural cheeses contain "real" ingredients: milk, rennin (a natural enzyme), and lactic acid bacteria (to sour the milk naturally). Swiss, provolone, Monterey Jack, Cheddar, and brick are examples of good, natural cheese.

ARROWROOT

Arrowroot is a tasteless, white powder that can be used as a thickening for gravies and sauces. It may be substituted in equal amounts for cornstarch or white flour (both are bleached products). It is easily digestible and also adds minerals.

BAKING POWDER

Double-acting baking powder contains aluminum compounds, whereas single-acting baking powder contains an acidic ingredient (tartaric acid) and baking soda. Researchers have been concerned for many years about the possible toxicity in consuming aluminum in our foods. To be on the safe side, use the single-acting kind.

PEANUT BUTTER

Natural peanut butter contains peanuts and sometimes salt. Most brands found on your grocer's shelf are hydrogenated (artificially hardened) to help keep the peanut oil from separating. Sweeteners also are added to commercially prepared peanut butter. A quick stir of the jar of natural peanut butter makes everything look fine and your family comes out ahead.

SAFFLOWER MAYONNAISE

Most supermarket mayonnaise contains preservatives and additives. If you don't want to make your own, purchase safflower mayonnaise to use in your favorite recipes.

PROTEIN

Using grains, legumes, and milk products in proper combination is a healthy replacement for meat. Livestock raised for human consumption too frequently contains unacceptable levels of toxic pesticides and herbicides, antibiotics, or synthetic hormones. (See *Infant Nutrition* chapter for additional information about non-meat alternatives.)

NATURAL CEREALS

Can breakfast exist without sugar-coated, artificially colored cereals? Fortunately, the answer is "yes." There are two general choices.

The first is to buy prepared cereals in a health food store or in the natural food section of your grocery store. Although several varieties exist, it still is necessary to read the labels. Do not assume it is natural, sugar-free, additive-free, or preservative-free just because you found it in the natural food section. (Check the list at the end of this chapter for suggestions.)

Making cereal from grains is easy and another way to provide baby and family with a wholesome breakfast. Oats, rice, and corn meal can be cooked into delicious cereals for baby. One packaged natural cereal we buy is a wheat cereal called "Bear Mush". Cleverly named and packaged (little bears on the package eating porridge) by Arrowhead Mills, this cereal is a real hit with children. "Bear Mush" sounds a lot more exciting than "Cream of Wheat"!

UNREFINED OILS

Unrefined oils include: safflower, sesame, soybean, corn, olive, peanut, and wheat germ oil. In the refinement of oil, Vitamin E is removed and preservatives added. Safflower oil is a mild, inexpensive, almost tasteless oil that can easily be substituted for any refined oil.

VANILLA EXTRACT

Imitation vanilla flavoring and vanillin are both artificial substitutes for pure vanilla. Using vanilla in recipes makes a distinct difference you will enjoy.

SEA SALT

Babies do not need salt. Children and adults do not need a lot of salt, especially if hypertension is a problem. Regular table salt contains anti-caking chemicals to keep the salt flowing freely and sodium bicarbonate to keep it white. Sea salt is just that; sea salt. It offers minerals that are taken out in the refining of table salt. Using herbs and spices and realizing that many foods naturally contain sodium can be one more step toward overall good health.

HONEY AND MOLASSES

Honey or molasses can be used to replace sugar in most recipes. Nutritional awareness has caused many parents to cut back the amount of sugar they give their children.

What is so bad about sugar? Sugar contributes nothing of nutritional value to the body; in fact, it takes away valuable

B-vitamins during the digestive process. Sugar also rots teeth. Sugar adds weight and can cause jangled nerves.

How can a sweet tooth be satisfied? We all seem to crave something sweet now and then. Fresh fruit contains natural sweeteners.

How can foods be sweetened without sugar? Honey is a great substitute because it is a natural product from the nectar of flowers. Because honey is sweeter than sugar, you need to use less sugar than is called for in a recipe. Honey causes baked foods to brown faster so baking time might need to be shortened. Decrease the amount of other liquids by one-fourth cup for each cup of honey used.

Molasses is another good sweetener. It is high in B-vitamins and a good source of calcium and iron.

YELLOW CORNMEAL

White cornmeal is degerminated, bleached, stripped of its original vitamins, and then synthetically enriched. Natural yellow cornmeal (labeled "unbolted") contains more Vitamin A than commercial, degerminated cornmeal.

WHOLE-WHEAT FLOUR

Whole-wheat flour contains Vitamin B and E, protein, iron, and phosphorus. It does not need to be "enriched" since nature already has done its job. The wheat bran and wheat germ are milled out of white flour, causing a loss of fiber. White flour also is bleached and enriched to synthetically replace some of the nutrients taken out during processing.

It is best to purchase whole-wheat flour in small quantities and store in the refrigerator to ensure freshness. If exposed to warm temperatures it can spoil eventually, causing a bad taste and odor.

For each cup of white flour needed, replace with ¾ cup whole-wheat flour. If white flour has been a part of your household for years, make the change gradually. First switch to unbleached flour (this is one step up from white flour since it was spared the bleaching process). Then try substituting ½ cup unbleached flour and ½ cup whole-wheat flour for each cup of white flour you once used. For most people this gradual change is easily accepted.

BROWN RICE

White rice is another example of a whole grain being robbed of its important nutrients. Brown rice is a nutritionally superior grain well worth the extra time it takes to prepare. Cooking time for brown rice is about 45 minutes, but it is good time invested in providing baby and the rest of your family with another natural, whole food. Brown rice freezes well so make extra and freeze in one cup portions for later use! Basmati rice is a "white" whole grain rice that cooks in 20 minutes and has a nice nutty flavor. It is a good substitute when moving from white rice to brown rice.

A Trip to the Health Food Store

If you plan to purchase many of the above foods for the first time, the most economical place is through a food cooperative or a health food store. Many large supermarkets now include a natural food section so that a special trip is not needed.

Have you avoided shopping in "health food" stores because they look different than your regular supermarket? Here a few tips to guide you through your first visit.

The biggest difference between a health food store and a regular supermarket is what is on the shelves. The wonderful bins of whole grains, beans, rice, dried fruits, and nuts are there for you to measure just how much you want. Because you, the consumer, do the measuring, bagging, and often price labeling, you are the one to pocket the savings. (Note — not all "health food" products are cheaper. Shop around and make sure you are not paying for pretty packaging or health food fads.) **Caution:** Be sure the health food store you choose maintains superior sanitary conditions. If you have any doubts as to the freshness or source of any foods — question the manager or return questionable items.

To many people, health food stores can be a bit intimidating. One way to become familiar with the store is to have a friend or neighbor take you with them on their next trip. If this isn't possible, stop in one day to just browse. Watch what people are doing, how they bag the food, if they are writing a price on the package, where things are, and what items cost. If you see something you want, measure what you need and march up to the cashier with your purchase. The next time you shop there, things will be more familiar. Most sales clerks are more than willing to help you — so go ahead and ask.

Good Foods for Baby or Toddler
A Supermarket* Shopper's Guide

FRUITS/JUICES:	SOME GOOD BRANDS
Applesauce	Any sugar-free 100% natural supermarket brands, Gathering Winds, Eden, Walnut Acres
Fruit juices	After the Fall, Lakewood, Eden, Juice Brothers, Walnut Acres, Tree of Life
Frozen grape juice	Seneca (sugar-free)

JAMS/SPREADS:	SOME GOOD BRANDS
Apple butter	Tap'n Apple, Baugher, Eden, Shiloh Farms
Peanut butter	Arrowhead Mills, Deaf Smith
Nut butters (sesame, almond, peanut, cashew)	Westbrae Natural, Sahadi, Joyva, Walnut Acres, Arrowhead Mills, Deaf Smith
Jams, fruit spreads	Whole Earth, Walnut Acres, Cascadian Farm, Sorrell Ridge

BREADS/CRACKERS:	SOME GOOD BRANDS
Rice cakes	Arden, Chico-San, Spiral
Chapati flat bread	Garden of Eden
Whole-wheat pita bread	Any 100% whole-wheat
Corn tortillas	Azteca
Biscuits for toddlers	Healthy Times
100% wheat crackers	Health Valley
Rye Norwegian Flatbread	Kavli
Original sesame crackers	Ak-mak
Crackers	Ryvita
Crisp bread	Wasa

DAIRY PRODUCTS:	SOME GOOD BRANDS
Yogurt	Alta Dena, Mountain High
Ice Cream	Haagen Dazs ice cream

CEREALS:	SOME GOOD BRANDS
Old-fashioned oats	Quaker
Puffed cereals (rice, wheat, millet, and corn)	El Molino
Crispy brown rice	New England Organic Produce Center, Erewhon
Nature O's	Arrowhead Mills
Oatios	New England Organic Produce Center
Swiss Baby Food Cereal	Muesli Familia
100% Natural Cereal	Familia
Golden Wheat Lites	Health Valley
Brown Rice Lites	Health Valley
Whole wheat flakes	Grainfield's
Bear Mush	Arrowhead Mills
7 Grain Cereal	Arrowhead Mills
Apple-Amaranth granola	Arrowhead Mills
Cream of rye	Con Agra
100% Natural Cereal For Babies	Health Valley
The Healthy Sweetener	Crawford's
Hearts O' Bran	Health Valley
Twelve Grain Cereal	Walnut Acres
Indian Meal Cereal	Walnut Acres
Good Shepherd (granola)	SoVex
Sprouts 7	Health Valley

*Most large supermarkets have a natural foods section. Be sure to ask the manager to order foods you need but do not see on the grocer's shelves.

Notes on Favorite Natural Foods

Product/Brand: **Purchased From:**

_____   _____

_____   _____

_____   _____

_____   _____

_____   _____

_____   _____

_____   _____

_____   _____

_____   _____

_____   _____

_____   _____

_____   _____

_____   _____

_____   _____

_____   _____

_____   _____

_____   _____

_____   _____

_____   _____

_____   _____

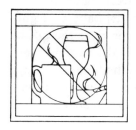

4 Into the Mouths of Future Moms

In the beginning, or even before the conception of your baby, nutrition plays a vital role in the creation of a healthy newborn. "Future moms" are increasingly aware that careful selection of wholesome foods is a real plus when aiming for a healthy baby. Months (even years) before conception, women are becoming selective about the food and drink they consume. Many prospective mothers take a good look at their bodies and wisely cut down on sugar, caffeine, alcohol, and smoking. They exercise to strengthen their bodies; the soon-to-be home of their offspring. The coffee and donut breakfast, missed lunch, and highly processed dinner are replaced by meals that provide quality in every bite. The future mom does this because of the realization that she is the one responsible for the nourishment that passes through her womb to the baby. Whewwww . . . heavy responsibility comes so soon when two join together to create another little mouth to feed!

One of the early concerns of a pregnant woman is weight gain. Most doctors or midwives recommend an average gain of between 25-35 pounds. The pattern of weight gain, as well as the amount, also is important. Many women dread this "heavier" part of pregnancy, thinking they just don't want to look fat. Don't worry though; luckily there is a BIG difference between being fat and being pregnant!

Being pregnant causes a woman to add a nice big bulge around the front of her body — there's another living creature inside! Breasts become larger as they begin to prepare for the very first (and home-made!) baby food. Without adding this roundness to the upper and lower parts of her body, it would be somewhat difficult to give birth!

When the baby pops out (oh, if only it were that simple!) a woman immediately loses about 10 pounds; baby's weight, placenta, plus some fluids. After the doctor gives the OK at the post-partum exam, a woman can gradually resume exercise and physical activities that will help to shed the remaining excess weight. If the woman chooses to nurse, her breasts will remain larger and the uterus returns to normal shape rather quickly.

The large roundness leads to a very special little human being with whom you get to share your life. Most women think the extra weight is a great trade for the end result!

What should a pregnant woman eat? Basically, the same wholesome foods required by healthy adults, but more of them. When pregnant, a woman *is* eating for two so what she eats or does not eat affects both mother and child. Baby's nutritional needs are taken care of first with any "extra" nutrients passed to the mother — so don't shortchange either of those two people!

The need for protein increases dramatically during pregnancy. The developing brain cells of the baby depend on constant protein intake. During the last three months of pregnancy, there occurs an even greater need for protein because of the baby's rapidly growing body. If a pregnant woman falls short of her required protein intake, toxemia could occur. This serious disease can be dangerous to both infant and mother, so constant pre-natal care is a must. This is why blood pressure, a warning signal of toxemia, is monitored closely during pre-natal exams.

During pregnancy, the body's need for calcium doubles (from 1,000 milligrams to 2,000 milligrams). Four glasses of skim milk in the daily diet is one way for pregnant women to obtain adequate amounts of calcium. Drinking skim milk also allows room for more calories in another part of the diet. If milk is not a favorite drink — cheese, leafy greens, and certain herbal teas can be substituted.

Along with increased protein and calcium needs, a pregnant woman must be careful to eat enough foods that contain iron. The growing fetus will be storing the iron needed for the first six months after birth. This is one of the reasons doctors prescribe the large vitamin-mineral pill pregnant women "love" to take daily. The iron contained in this supplement is a little added insurance to help meet nutritional requirements. The following foods are high in iron and can help prevent anemia (iron deficiency) during pregnancy: whole grains, beans, dark green vegetables, sunflower seeds, seafood, and molasses.

Folic acid (folicin) deficiency is another condition that often occurs. Along with protein, folic acid, a member of the vitamin B-complex, is being used to help form large amounts of baby's new tissues. So much is needed during pregnancy that the Recommended Daily Allowance is twice what is normally required (800 grams during pregnancy). The best natural sources of folic acid include carrots, egg yolk, dark green leafy vegetable, avocados, apricots, and whole-wheat flour.

Recently many doctors have discovered the ill-effects stress can cause the unborn baby. Stress seems to deplete B-vitamins so quickly it often causes a pregnant woman to become deficient in this very important group of vitamins. It is difficult to have a stress-free pregnancy, but every effort should be made to deal with stress by keeping a positive mental attitude and a good diet filled with B-vitamins.

Nausea is common complaint during the first three months of pregnancy. Many doctors now are prescribing a vitamin B-6 supplement and many mothers have reported good results. Eating smaller meals more often also seems to help prevent this unpleasant part of pregnancy.

In summary, baby becomes what mother does or does not eat. More nutrients are needed during pregnancy and lactation — especially protein, calcium iron, folic acid, and B-vitamins — than at any other time in life. Eating well is a nice way to show love for baby right from the start. A healthy mom is a nice present too!

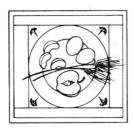

5 Infant Nutrition

Nutrition involves your body's use of the food you eat.

This simple statement helps remind parents of the important responsibility of choosing foods for their baby. No two babies have the exact same nutritional requirements. Age, sex, weight, physical activity, climate, and environment all must be considered to determine specific dietary needs.

As parents begin the process of making baby's food and planning wholesome meals for their offspring, a quick review of nutrition is in order. Instant recall of what foods have which vitamins is not necessary, but an overall picture of a few basics will help.

Remember learning about the basic four food groups in high school health class? Today, as parents, those food categories take on a more important meaning; especially as we begin to menu-plan for baby.

Take a quick look at the Basic Four food charts on pages 52, 53, and 54. Included are three different charts:

> Basic Four Food Groups
> Meatless Basic Four Food Groups
> Allergy Basic Four Food Groups

Choose the one (or two) needed for your family, and put a copy on your refrigerator door. You now are one step closer to insuring your baby is fed well. Organizing meals should be a bit easier.

Note the differences on the Meatless Basic Four chart and the Basic Four chart. A person on a lacto-ovo vegetarian diet should choose 6 daily servings from the grain-legumes-nuts-seeds group to replace the 2 servings of meat and 4 servings from the grain group in the Basic Four chart. Vegetarians also need to choose additional fruits and vegetables in order to obtain the proper balance of foods.

If you decide to feed your child a meatless diet, or are changing to a meat-free diet yourself, you must become familiar with the Meatless Basic Four. Protein requirements for baby (or anyone) on a vegetarian diet are met easily if the menu is properly planned. The rapid cell growth in the brain (and entire body) during early life makes it essential to have enough protein in order to achieve optimum development.

The best way to obtain protein without eating meat is to combine certain incomplete proteins. The proper combining of various protein foods is known as complementary proteins. Proper combinations of these foods eaten during the same meal can meet the same protein requirements contained in meat or eggs.

Animal products, fish, and soybeans have all eight of the essential amino acids necessary for use in our body. Because these amino acids are in "ready-to-use" form, many people tend to think of milk and eggs as perfect protein foods. Fortunately, it has been discovered that other foods are made up of incomplete plant proteins: legumes, dried peas and beans, dairy products, grains, nuts, and seeds. The proper combination of any of these food groups forms a complete protein. A few examples of dishes containing complementary proteins include: rice and bean casserole, corn tortillas and beans, whole grain cereals and milk, falafel (garbanzo beans with sesame seeds in a mixture), whole-wheat pizza (whole-wheat and cheese), enchilada bake (corn, beans, and cheese), lentil soup topped with cheese, and peanut butter balls (peanuts and non-fat dry milk). These dishes are economical, and baby has an easier time with digestion.

See the chart on page 51 for suggestions on food combinations that form complete proteins. For more information about protein complementarity, *Diet for a Small Planet,* by Frances Moore Lappé, is an excellent source.

There are several different kinds of vegetarians. The use of the word "vegetarian" in this cookbook means a diet containing no meat, but including dairy products and eggs. This is a "liberal" form of vegeterianism. Some people in this category occasionally include poultry or fish in their diet as well. One choosing these foods is known as a Lacto-Ovo vegetarian.

The opposite type of vegetarian is called a Vegan. Vegans obtain their proteins from plant sources only, and do not eat any dairy products. A note of caution: one following this type of diet must take a Vitamin B-12 supplement, because this vitamin is scarce in the vegan's food selection.

Another type of vegeterian is the Lacto-Vegetarian. This person eats dairy products, but no eggs (and of course no meats).

A note of caution to people (often teenagers) who declare themselves to be vegetarians, but unfortunately do not choose proper protein foods for their diet. If a person sits down to a "regular" meal with meat, potatoes, and vegetables and avoids meat, protein requirements will not be met. Worse yet is the choice of an entirely meatless, but highly process diet. If you know a so-called "vegetarian" in this category, please share this information about protein complementarity with that person.

The Allergy Basic Four chart is a guide for substituting different foods in place of those containing milk, eggs, wheat, or corn. All four are common causes of food allergy. You will note that non-milk products replace foods in the Basic Four milk group. If your child is allergic to wheat or corn, adaptations can be made when selecting foods from the grain group.

Keeping a written daily tally of each food ingested is time-consuming and unnecessary if you are using any one of the Basic Four charts as a guide to planning meals. However, the first few times your baby has three meals a day, you might want to chart the items eaten under the various food groups. This may help in your menu-planning and ensure that your baby is eating foods from the various food groups.

Nutrients

Along with knowledge of the Four Food groups, we need to take a look at the kinds of nutrients needed for baby's energy, growth, and development.

Your baby will grow faster during the first year than at any other time in life. A healthy, growing baby needs the same number of nutrients as an adult, but in lesser amounts. There are over 45 nutrients divided into 6 classifications:

Protein	Vitamins
Carbohydrates	Minerals
Fats and Oils	Water

Protein

Protein is essential for the rapid growth, development, and repair of all body tissues (muscles, blood, glands, heart, brain, nerves, and skin). Next to water, it makes up the largest portion (approximately 15-20 percent) of body weight. Protein also is needed in the formation of enzymes (to aid digestion), hormones (to regulate many body functions), and antibodies. A lack of protein can cause growth to be retarded and also lower resistance to disease and infections. Since protein is not stored by the body, baby needs adequate amounts of protein each day.

Carbohydrates

Carbohydrates are known to us in the form of sugar, starch, and cellulose, providing baby with most of the total calories needed for heat and energy. As the major source of immediate energy and also the energy source for the brain and nervous system, they obviously are important to baby's diet. Carbohydrates aid the body in the use of protein and fat, but many carbohydrates will end up being stored in the body as fat. On the other hand, if the carbohydrate intake is too low, the body must use them for fuel rather than for growth. Cellulose is the indigestible carbohydrate found in many vegetables and fruits. Carbohydrates should make up about 60 percent of baby's diet and should be eaten in the least refined form for optimum benefit.

Natural starch sources:

Bananas	Pasta
Cereals	Peas
Corn	Potatoes
Dried peas and beans	Winter squash

Natural sugar sources:

Apples	Oranges
Bananas	Peas
Carrots	Honey
Grapes	

Fats and Oils

Contrary to popular opinion, not all fats are bad! Fats and oils are needed to ensure good usage of proteins and carbohydrates. They also provide the body with a reserve energy supply. Without enough fat in the diet, baby would need to burn up protein for energy.

There are more good things to say about fats! They help to delay hunger, add flavor to foods, and aid in the absorption of the fat-soluble vitamins A, D, E, and K. Stored fats are essential in providing a constant body temperature and they help protect the internal organs from injury.

The essential fatty acids found in fats and oils are important for baby's growth and for maintaining healthy skin. Essential fatty acids are: linoleic acid, linolenic acid, and arachidonic acid. Of these three, linoleic acid is most important.

Good sources of linoleic acids include:

Breast milk   Safflower oil
Avocados   Sesame oil
Soybeans   Sunflower oil
Sunflower seeds   Soy oil
Sesame seeds

Baby can get fats and oils needed from natural foods such as:

Low-fat dairy products
Grains
Avocados
Soybeans
Peanut butter
Sesame seeds (ground)
Sunflower seeds (ground)

Vitamins

The delicate balance between health and disease often is dependent on what vitamins are consumed and used properly by our bodies. Vitamins, in their natural state, are small, organic substances found in foods that are necessary for life. Babies eating a variety of natural foods usually have little problem getting enough vitamins.

Natural vitamin supplements, usually in pill form, are also found in food. Synthetic vitamins and natural vitamins have the same chemical analysis. However, a synthetically derived vitamin can cause toxic reactions in some susceptible people while the same vitamin in natural form is tolerated. Some authorities believe there are less gastrointestinal upsets with natural vitamin supplements.

Authorities differ on the necessity of vitamin supplements. Some say that if the diet is proper, there is no additional need. Others, while encouraging a good diet, believe that various factors (stress, disease, smoking, medications) cause more vitamins to be used by the body and leave people with a detrimental shortage of vitamins. Eating processed foods poor in vitamins also can cause deficiencies.

Although all the nutrients humans need can be obtained by eating a good balance of whole and natural foods, it must be mentioned that foods grown in today's soil are not as rich in vitamins and other nutrients as they were 100 years ago. Increased pollution of air, soil, and water causes food sources to be more contaminated than in the past. Therefore, vitamin supplements, taken properly and with good meals and under doctor supervision, can insure a healthy level of vitamins in the body.

Name That Vitamin

There are 2 types of vitamins:

Water-soluble — (B complex and C)
Fat-soluble — (A, D, E, and K)

Water-soluble vitamins are not stored in the body and, therefore, need to be replaced daily.

The fat-soluble vitamins are stored in the body. They cannot be found harmful in the foods we eat. However, if too many vitamin supplements of A, D, E, and K are taken — they can be harmful.

Remember — vitamins are not substitutes for foods nor are they pep pills. They have no caloric or energy value of their own. If vitamins are consumed without proper diet, good health will disappear!

For example, an overdose of Vitamin A can result in:

Nausea	Blurred vision
Vomiting	Rashes
Bone pain	Fatigue
Hair loss	Liver enlargement

or, excessive Vitamin D can cause:

> Too much calcium to be absorbed and removed from bones, thereby causing deposits to form that possibly could damage the heart, lungs, and blood vessels.

> Nausea, vomiting, dizziness, diarrhea, can occur if large amounts are taken too suddenly.

Vitamin A
(fat-soluble)

Function: necessary for growth, good eyesight, strong bones, healthy skin, teeth, gums, and hair. Helps baby to build resistance against respiratory infections.

Good sources:

Carrots	Milk
Eggs	Dairy products
Fish liver oil	Breast milk
Green and yellow vegetables	Liver
Yellow fruits	Kidney

Vitamin B Complex
(water-soluble)

Function: allows body to obtain energy from carbohydrates. Promotes growth, healthy appetite and skin, and aids in digestive process. Essential for keeping good balance in nervous system.

Good sources:

Brewer's yeast	Leafy green vegetables
Wheat germ	Breast milk
Wheat bran	Milk
Nuts	Brown rice
Dried beans and peas	Cheese
Soybeans	Egg yolk
Pork	Bananas
Organ meats	Lentils
Fish	Peanut butter
Poultry	

Vitamin C
(water-soluble)

Function: needed by the body cells for growth; repair of body tissues, strong bones, teeth, gums, and blood vessels. Helps body absorb iron.

Good sources:

Citrus fruits
Green and leafy vegetables
Breast milk
Potatoes
Sweet potatoes
Tomatoes

Vitamin D
(the fat-soluble sunshine vitamin!)

Functions: essential to baby's bone formation by providing proper utilization of calcium and phosphorus. Important for good teeth.

Good sources:

Sunlight
Milk
Dairy products
Fish liver oils
Salmon
Tuna
Herring
Sardines

Vitamin E
(fat-soluble)

Functions: necessary for cellular growth, helping promote endurance and alleviating fatigue. Provides protection against air pollution and is especially helpful for babies.

Good sources:

Breast milk
Wheat germ oil
Peanut oil
Soy oil
Whole grains
Wheat germ
Brussel sprouts
Leafy greens
Spinach
Nuts
Eggs

Vitamin K
(fat-soluble)

Function: essential for proper clotting of blood; i.e., allowing tissue to form over cuts and scrapes.

Good sources:

Breast milk	Soybean oil
Alfalfa	Leafy green vegetables
Yogurt	Cauliflower
Egg yolk	Kelp
Safflower oil	Cabbage

Minerals

Minerals are elements contained in each cell in your body. They regulate certain vital bodily functions. Although minerals comprise only four percent of the body weight — they are an extremely important nutrient.

Minerals found in the body are primarily calcium, phosphorus, sodium, potassium, and magnesium. These other minerals are also essential for your baby's growth:

Chlorine	Selenium
Chromium	Sodium
Cobalt	Sulfur
Copper	Vanadium
Iodine	Zinc
Manganese	

Calcium

Function: More calcium is in the body than any other mineral (most of it can be found in the bones and teeth in an adult). Important for health, formation of bones and teeth.

Good sources:

Cheese	Sardines
Dried beans	Sesame seeds
Green vegetables	Sunflower seeds
Peanuts	Soybeans
Salmon	Walnuts

Phosphorus

Function: properly balanced with calcium it helps with bone and teeth formation, and also helps muscle, nerve, and kidney function.

Good sources:

Whole grain	Fish
Eggs	Poultry
Nuts	Meat
Seeds	Red Cabbage

Sodium

Function: essential for normal growth; works with potassium to regulate the amount of water in and around body cells. Helps nerves and muscles to function properly.

Good sources:

Salt	Bacon
Beets	Dried beef
Carrots	Brains
Artichokes	Kidney
	Shellfish

Potassium

Function: works well with sodium to regulate proper water balance in the body. Helps regulate blood flow to make the heart pump efficiently, and works with magnesium in synthesizing protein. Combines with phosphorus to send oxygen to the brain.

Good sources:

Bananas
Citrus fruits
Dried beans
Green leafy vegetables
Sunflower seeds
Potatoes
Mint leaves

Magnesium

Function: necessary for efficient nerve and muscle functions, strong bones and teeth, and allowing the enzymes in the body to work properly.

Good sources:

Almonds	Apples
Figs	Lemons
Nuts	Seeds
Dark green vegetables	Yellow corn
Dried beans and peas	Whole grains

Water

Water is the most important nutrient (although authorities often differ as to whether or not water is a nutrient). Because of its obvious importance to the body tissues and functions, it is included here. At least one half of the body's weight actually is water. The human body cannot live longer than a few days without this important nutrient.

Babies get most of their water from drinking water, eating fruits, vegetables, and fruit juices. This water is necessary for digestion, removing body wastes, and regulating the body temperature.

Babies lose water daily through urine (confirmed by the never-ending diaper changes), bowel movements (lots of those, too), and also through perspiration. Vomiting and diarrhea also cause water loss. Dehydration can occur in infants more readily than in adults, so be sure baby's liquid intake is adequate. Heslin (*No-Nonsense Nutrition for Your Baby's First Year*) suggests a guideline of one-third cup be given for each pound of the baby's weight until the total reaches six cups per day.

A breast-fed baby gets plenty of water through mother's milk, according to Karen Pryor in *Nursing Your Baby*. She suggests the mother should drink more water during hot weather; not the baby. Of course, an occasional bottle of water can be given during the first 6 months of nursing when juices have not yet been introduced. Formula-fed babies need bottles of water to help the kidneys in eliminating the proteins and salts, found in cow's milk, which are not used by the human body.

Obesity

Overfeeding our infant should not be considered a sign of our affection. With the creation of fat babies, we could also be creating fat adults. Those with weight problems would certainly wish not to have the number of fat cells in existence. Fat cells created during infancy (and some authorities believe more develop during adolescence) are the same number that hold fat later on in life. In other words, once fat cells develop, the number never decreases. The amount of fat stored in the body is determined by this number of fat cells.

Approximately 20 percent of our children are obese. The number of fat cells present in the bodies of these children will never disappear. Eating less food and getting more exercise can cause some of this fat to burn up (expend calories) and reduce the size of the fat cells — but the numbers will always be there.

As parents, we must do all we can to avoid overfeeding and under-exercising our children. Don't put food in baby's mouth everytime he or she cries. Let baby explore the world around him with you there for safety. Keep "confined time" to a minimum. Babies should not spend most of their day in a playpen or high chair. Remember that overfeeding is not a sign of love. Keep baby active and well-fed — but not OVERFED!

Obesity is a numbers game — and the overweight children are the losers . . . everywhere except on the scale. Let's look at the numbers. An infant is born with 5 to 6 billion fat cells. These cells multiply to 30 to 40 billion by normal adulthood. Eating too much with little physical activity can cause fat cells to increase in number. Therefore, an obese adult, who was overweight as a child, might end up with 80 to 120 billion fat cells. Although these fat cells are of normal size — that is *far too many* of them. In contrast, if a person gains weight as an adult, the fat cells already in existence grow larger but the numbers stay constant. Overweight adults who were overweight children find it almost impossible to reduce their weight permanently.

The overall selection of foods (with emphasis on proper combination of protein foods to achieve complementarity in a meatless diet) is important to keep in mind when menu-planning. Moderation, variety, and the wholesomeness of the foods chosen should provide your child with optimum nutrition.

Establishing good eating habits and good exercise habits at an early age will help our children get off to a **good,** healthy start in life. Exercise is important to all of us, but especially our young. It helps establish good habits for the future. Walk, run, swim, jump, skip, dance, and stretch with your child. The rewards are multifold!

Food Combinations that Form Complete Proteins

	Corn	Beans/legumes	Milk	Peanuts	Potatoes	Rice	Sesame seed	Soybeans	Sunflower seeds	Wheat
Beans or legumes	●		●			●	●			●
Corn		●								
Corn & milk								●		
Corn & soy			●							
Milk		●		●	●	●	●			●
Milk & peanuts										●
Peanuts			●						●	
Peanuts & sesame seeds								●		
Rice		●	●							
Rice & wheat								●		
Sesame seeds		●	●							
Sesame seeds & soy				●						●
Sesame seeds & wheat								●		
Sunflower seeds				●						
Wheat		●	●							
Wheat & milk				●						
Wheat & peanuts			●							
Wheat & soy						●				

Basic Four Food Groups
(for diets that include meat)

Food Group	Servings*	Food Sources
Dairy	3	milk cheese butter yogurt

Fruits and Vegetables	4	**Dark green, leafy, or other vegetables**
		green beans spinach carrots
		peas kale squash
		green pepper lettuce pumpkin
		zucchini cabbage corn
		broccoli tomatoes
		    cauliflower
		    potatoes
		
		Citrus fruits **Sweet fruits**
		oranges peaches bananas
		lemons pears avocados
		limes apricots apples
		grapefruits grapes
		tangerines
		pineapples

Meat/Protein	2	beef fish poultry eggs complementary protein combinations
Grains	4	rice oats rye millet barley bran corn cereals breads pasta

* Serving size will be smaller for infants, larger for adults, and a bit larger for pregnant or lactating women and teens.

Meatless Basic Four Food Groups
(for lacto-ovo vegetarian diets)

Food Group	Servings	Food Sources	
Dairy	3	milk cheese eggs yogurt	
Fruits	1-4	**Citrus** oranges lemons limes grapefruits tangerines pineapples	**Sweet** peaches pears apricots grapes bananas avocados apples
Vegetables	3	green beans peas green pepper zucchini broccoli spinach kale lettuce	cabbage carrots squash pumpkin corn tomatoes cauliflower potatoes
Grains **Legumes** **Nuts** **Seeds**	6	**Grains,** rice, oats, rye, millet, barley, corn **Legumes,** garbanzo beans, dry beans, dry peas, lentils **Nuts,** peanuts, almonds, walnuts **Seeds,** sesame, sunflower	

Allergy Basic Four Food Groups
(for those with food allergies)

Food Group	Servings	Food Sources
Dairy	3	**(Milk or egg-free diet)** milk-free formula soy milk nut milk (as recommended by physician)
Fruits and Vegetables	4	any fruit or vegetable not causing allergic reactions (watch out for citrus fruits)
Meat/Protein	2	meat fish poultry (as recommended by physician)
Grains	4	**(Wheat-free or corn-free diet)** rice millet arrowroot oats rice flour oat flour barley flour potato flour rye flour soy flour

6 Feeding Your Baby

To breast feed or not to breast feed, that is the first question to be answered! This choice ultimately is made by the mother after considering the advantages and the disadvantages of breast feeding and bottle feeding while keeping in mind her present lifestyle.

The awesome experience of nursing both of our children tends to make me lean toward encouraging all mothers to at least try breast feeding. Breast feeding provides a special bond between mother and child, creating an inner peace and intense joy that is wonderfully overwhelming.

The choice to breast feed is made knowing that the mother must always (or almost always) be available for the infant. Many mothers use a breast pump to save their own milk and freeze it for use when they are not available at feeding time. Karen Pryor's book, *Nursing Your Baby*, provides valuable information for any woman who is considering breast feeding. The LaLeche League in your area is a wonderful support group available for additional information.

It is very important for the nursing mother to maintain a good diet to ensure optimum nutritional benefits from her milk. If the mother eats a well-balanced diet, she will pass on to her baby adequate amounts of essential vitamins. A nursing mother expends approximately 1,000 calories per day while nursing her baby. This factor is often helpful in regaining or improving on the pre-pregnancy weight of the mother. (Be careful not to skimp on nutritional needs at this time though!)

Breast feeding also brings with it certain responsibilities. The decision to breast feed is made knowing that the mother must be readily available for her baby. The mother must make sure her diet is one of quality, to provide her and the baby

MEATLESS BASIC FOUR FOOD GROUPS

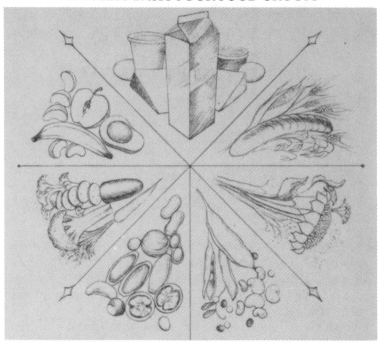

BASIC FOUR FOOD GROUPS

with necessary nutrients. Making this decision also can bring with it the disapproval of parents, friends, or relatives. Fortunately, the recent increase in the number of nursing mothers has helped in the acceptance of this beautiful and natural way of feeding our offspring.

Many parents have found that a combination of formula feeding and breast feeding works best for them. It gives the father a special time to be with the baby at meal time and frees the mother for a more flexible schedule.

If the decision is made to bottle feed — for whatever reason — don't let any nursing mothers make you feel uncomfortable with your decision. Part of their enthusiasm for nursing often spills over into a religious-type fervor that prompts them to "spread the word" as to how wonderful breast feeding is for everyone. It isn't wonderful for everyone in every situation! Make a realistic decision as to what is best for *you*.

If you decide to bottle feed, be sure to choose an iron fortified formula (with the pediatrician's help). It is essential that all bottles, nipples, and utensils are clean. These are other helpful hints for parents who are feeding their baby formula:

- Make a one-day supply of formula at a time and throw away unused formula at the end of the day.
- If you choose a ready-to-drink formula, do not add any water. (This type is more expensive, but convenient for traveling).
- Never force baby to finish a bottle. Heed the baby's signals when he attempts to "tell" you he is finished!
- Never prop a bottle — this could cause choking. Holding your baby close helps make feeding times a warmer experience for baby and the person feeding him.
- Follow the pediatrician's advice as to how much formula to give your baby.
- Be sure to ask the doctor for proper vitamin supplements during these early feeding times also.

Most authorities suggest waiting to make the switch from bottle or breast to whole milk until age one. For this reason, formula or breast milk is used in all the recipes for babies under age one.

The decision to breast feed or formula feed your baby should be given a lot of thought. If you are uncertain as to which way you want to go, do some thorough research. Read some of the books listed in the Bibliography and discuss both options with your doctor and mate.

Breast Feeding

ADVANTAGES:

Mother-infant bonding is very strong
Breast milk is nature's most perfect food
Said to aid in preventing certain allergies and decrease chances of ear infection
Said to give some protection against disease
Helps uterus shrink faster
More economical
Baby's need to suck is naturally satisfied
Timesaving — time is not needed to prepare formula or clean bottles
Easy to travel with a nursing baby
Milk is always available if mother eats properly
Milk is always the proper temperature
No formula stain on baby's clothing
Infant utilizes the protein in the breast milk with maximum efficiency
Little danger of baby being overfed
Baby's stools do not have an unpleasant odor

DISADVANTAGES:

Mother must be available at feeding time
Father has little part in feeding
Possibility of negative attitude from family and friends
Cannot easily leave baby for prolonged amount of time

Bottle Feeding

ADVANTAGES:

More convenient in some ways because baby can be fed a bottle by anyone — not just the mother
Frees the mother if time is needed away from home
Father or siblings can have more involvement with feedings

DISADVANTAGES:

Time needed to sterilize and prepare bottles
Odor of baby's stool is strong and unpleasant
Possibility of overfeeding
Propped bottles of milk can lead to tooth decay

That Big Day . . . Starting Solids!

Between the ages of four and six months, your baby will begin to show signs that milk is not enough to satisfy his hunger. When his appetite noticeably increases or when he begins to reach for food at the family table, these are good indications that your baby is ready to start solid foods. Current recommendations on starting solids suggest you wait until the baby is between 4-6 months old. Some authorities believe that the closer to six months, the better. This philosophy is reflected in the recipe section of this book.

Once a baby starts on a solid diet, the parents have the task of choosing the foods that will supply their baby with essential vitamins and minerals. Since there are many differing views on the necessity for vitamin supplements, consult your child's pediatrician or a preventive medicine specialist.

By six months of age the iron supply a baby is born with will almost be depleted so it is important to make sure iron is included in your baby's diet. Because cereal is a good source of iron, it often is the first "solid" food to be introduced. Choose a rice or oat cereal — wait to give any wheat cereal until 8 months or so because many babies will have an allergic reaction if this food is introduced too early.

The first feeding should be just a spoonful or two (try to avoid the urge to make enough for all the kids on the block!), offered gently, for the baby to experiment with the new sensation. This will be an entirely new experience for your baby so try not to rush things. Baby can be fed from a small baby chair, on your lap, or securely and comfortably in a high chair. It doesn't matter whether the cereal is offered for breakfast or lunch — it probably is best to choose a non-fussy time of day when baby is contented.

Offer the same food all week, gradually increasing the amount to about three to four tablespoons. The next week, offer another cereal or a fruit. Mashed, ripe banana is a real favorite, with a nice taste that most babies will enjoy. The amount of food served will vary from baby to baby and slowly increase with age. Use your good judgment and let your baby help to guide you. Babies' instincts are very interesting! They usually know when they are hungry and when to stop eating. (Some adults would love to have these instincts still!)

Soon banana and rice cereal can be combined for a meal or offer cereal for breakfast and banana for lunch. Juice can be introduced for snack time. (Try offering juice occasionally in a small spouted cup. Babies catch on quickly, and it's good for babies to try new things). Diluted apple juice or strained orange juice usually is well liked. Don't buy the baby food juice unless you want to pay extra. Check labels on the apple juice, and choose a juice made of apples and water and nothing else. Choose a frozen orange juice with nothing extra added, or fresh squeeze your own juice if you want. Be sure to pour the juice through a strainer for baby's initial feedings; this will catch the strands of pulp that often make a baby gag.

Gradually introduce a variety of fruits and cereals over a two-month period. Avocados, cooked apples, pears, peaches, papaya, and apricots, are fruits to choose. Check the recipe section for preparation.

All foods should be puréed and portions kept small. Start with one meal a day the first few weeks, then gradually go to two meals. Keep in mind your child's individual needs, and watch for signs of hunger or overfeeding. It is especially important to only offer one new food per week. If any allergic reaction should occur (rash, diarrhea, or irritability), it is more easily pinpointed when foods are offered in this manner.

Whole milk yogurt is an excellent food to be offered at around six months. Yogurt is a nutritious food highly noted for its abundance of B vitamins and for its beneficial effects to the digestive system. It is interesting to note that this whole milk product is usually tolerated so well at this age when whole milk itself is not recommended for a baby before age one. The reason is this: the fermenting process of the milk breaks down the lactose (milk sugar) into lactic acid. Therefore, that step in the digestive process is already completed by the time it reaches the stomach, making yogurt more acceptable to a baby with a milk intolerance. However, if you suspect your child has a milk allergy (rather than a milk intolerance), yogurt should *not* be given. When in doubt about a suspected milk allergy or intolerance, get advice from the pediatrician.

You might want to invest in a yogurt maker or borrow one from a friend (thanks, Sarah!). You can make five containers of yogurt with very little time, effort, or expense. All you need (besides the yogurt maker) is four (4) cups of milk and one (1) tablespoon of whole milk yogurt. It's worth checking into if you think you would eat the yogurt.

At around seven months, vegetables can be introduced (one a week, of course). It is easy to prepare larger batches of carrots, beans, peas, or squash and freeze them for easy use later. Fresh, cooked vegetables will have the maximum amount of vitamins and minerals, so it's nice to give baby a portion of fresh vegetables any time the family is eating them. Just purée them in the blender or baby food grinder. More grain cereals also can be introduced at around seven months of age. Try millet or barley cereal.

At eight months, baby begins to see a lot of options. Cooked egg yolk is good to offer at this time. Natural cheeses (avoid artificially made or colored cheeses) are usually loved by the eight-month old. Stronger vegetables such as cabbage, broccoli, and spinach, can be puréed for baby.

Nine months and a few teeth later, foods can be a bit lumpier, and the variety in the food groups broadens. Dry beans (garbanzo, lentils, pinto, soy, etc.) can be cooked, mashed, and given to baby. Peanut butter can be mashed with banana and mixed with formula or breast milk. Be sure the mixture is very thin to avoid gagging. Bulghur, wheat cereal, and more juices (grape, grapefruit, apricot), can be introduced. Tiny bite size pieces of soft foods can be offered. Put newspaper or an old plastic tablecloth under the high chair, and don't worry about the mess your baby makes at this time. Many people get into the habit of never allowing their baby to feed himself or make a mess trying. This is what we're here for; one of our jobs is to let our babies have successes and failures! They'll never learn to eat until we let them *try, slop,* and *spill.* I'm not advocating letting your two-year old daughter finger paint on her tray with applesauce, but it is important that we give a nine-month old the chance to reach his mouth. Give him a spoon, let him try.

Without sounding contradictory, it is important to remember that sometimes our children sense that we are preparing them for great independence. They go through spells when they really prefer to have Mommy or Daddy shovel the food in for them. On this matter — indulge! They are just testing to see if we still will take that time with them. They seem sometimes to be saying that they need that time. Someone once said, "They're only young once." So true.

A Basic Philosophy of Feeding

Each of us has our likes and dislikes — and so do babies! By keeping this in mind and by making mealtimes as relaxed as possible, our babies will enjoy feeding times and so will you.

Never force your baby (or older child) to eat a certain food or even a certain amount of food. Babies are quite intelligent and instinctive about what they need to eat. As long as wholesome food is available for your baby to choose from, he will do just fine.

There are parents who hated the fact that they were forced to eat certain foods when they were little, but find themselves doing the same thing to their children. This cycle should be broken — for everyone's sake.

Babies' tastes will change. Just when you think Katie has formed a lifelong love affair with peas — the next day she'll refuse to eat them! Don't hassle. Don't panic. Quietly set aside the peas, and offer them again a few days later.

Relax and enjoy baby's mealtime. Don't force your baby to eat. Respect your baby's tastes as you would have someone respect yours. Mealtimes will be a pleasure for everyone.

A word about grandparents. Just as we are learning to be good parents, our parents are working hard to be good grandparents. In their own way of trying to help us out, they often want to share their ideas on feeding, and are upset or bewildered that we may have chosen a ''different'' way to feed our baby. Breast feeding is a great example. Many mothers who raised children during the 40's, 50's, and 60's are appalled that someone would want to be bothered with breast feeding. To many, it is even embarrassing. If you have chosen to breast feed, keep in mind that our mothers went through a great media blitz that convinced them that formula was better than breast milk and much more convenient. They were told that a good modern mother feeds her baby formula if she wants him to grow big and strong. Imagine the shock or surprise when her daughter chooses to refute all this and decides to breast feed! ''Are you sure he's getting enough to eat?'' ''How do you know how many ounces she drank?'' ''She's crying — see there — she's still hungry.'' Many a well-meaning grandparent has been known to utter these words. If you are truly comfortable and confident in your decision to breast feed, let all these comments go over your head. Getting angry or defensive doesn't help. A quiet, peaceful response to the questions will go much further to keep family peace.

This holds true for the type of food you choose to give your baby also. Pre-packaged, processed, longer shelf-life foods were reported to be such wonderful things when our parents fed us. They chose to feed us the best way they knew how —just as we choose to feed our baby the most nutritious foods we can. There was little research done at that time concerning the ill effects of too much sugar, white flour, and processed foods. So remember that our parents may, at first, feel a bit threatened by our knowledge of nutrition and our different ideas about baby food. A calm and frank discussion about how you made your decisions about feeding and how your parents (or friends) made theirs might ease any tension that has occurred. Also, a quiet "thank you" might be nice to parents who have given wholehearted support for the important decisions we are making on how we have chosen to feed our baby (thanks, Mom and Dad)!

A word here about "deviating" from an entirely natural, unprocessed, whole food diet. We try as hard as we can to plan, cook, and provide healthy meals and snacks for our children. However, we have come to realize that we do not have total control over what goes into the mouths of our babes and children day in and day out. While doing our best to have wholesome food in our kitchen, we have learned not to get hysterical if our child had a cupcake or a piece of candy at a birthday party in school. Our belief is that if we make these foods "forbidden" we are setting our children up for failure. They cannot possibly comply with this expectation all the time. Therefore, we have educated our children quietly on the topics of nutrition, protein sources, hazards of sugar and processed food, and the differences between "good" food and food with little nutritional value. We allow *some* "junk" food *some* of the time. (It is never offered as a reward for good behavior — that would not make sense if we tell them to eat good food because we care about their health!) Those times are infrequent and we try hard to achieve a good balance in our daily diet. In other words, we believe a little bit of "non-perfect" food is not going to hurt in the overall view of things. However, if my child was hyperactive, diabetic, hypoglycemic, or had some other suspected or diagnosed medical problem, those deviations from an excellent diet would be too risky and not worth the price the child would pay. As a parent, *you* need to make the choices and educate your child according to *your* beliefs and lifestyles to provide balance in your family's life.

That First Year . . .
A Time Table* For Introducing Solid Foods

Food	4-6 months	7	8	9	10	11	12	Not until Age 2
Apple juice	●							
Applesauce	●							
Avocado	●							
Banana	●							
Barley	●							
Beets		●						
Berries[1]								●
Broccoli			●					
Bulghur			●					
Cabbage			●					
Carrots		●						
Cottage cheese	●							
Cheese			●					
Egg white							●	
Egg yolk			●					
Green beans		●						
Honey[2] (uncooked)							●	
Legumes				●				
Milk (cow's)[3]							●	
Millet	●							
Nuts, seeds (whole)							●	
Oats (oatmeal)	●							
Orange juice							●	
Papaya	●							
Peaches		●						
Peanut butter			●					
Pears	●							

Food	4-6 months	7	8	9	10	11	12	Not until Age 2
Peas		●						
Potato (mashed)			●					
Rice	●							
Spinach			●					
Sprouts (ground)			●					
Squash		●						
Sweet potato	●							
Tofu			●					
Tomato							●	
Yogurt	●							
Zucchini		●						

* This table contains information on suggested starting dates for various foods. Keep in mind that a baby should receive only one (1) new food a week — and giving baby every food listed under each month is not recommended.

[1] Puréed berries can be offered gradually after 12 months. Whole berries still can cause gagging so be careful and consider how well your child chews his food. Some berries cause diaper rash or skin rashes, so just be aware.

[2] Uncooked honey has caused botulism and even death in children under age one. Do NOT feed infants uncooked honey before age 1!

[3] Milk in this cookbook refers to breast milk or formula until age one (1). Authorities differ on starting dates for whole milk — some say it's okay at 6 months, and others suggest waiting until age one (1). I used milk in recipes that needed cooking or baking (i.e. pancakes, rice pudding, breads, after the age of 7 months, but used breast milk (you can use formula) for drinking "straight." Follow the pediatrician's advice on when to start giving your child milk, and watch closely for any allergic symptoms or reactions. Many infants just cannot tolerate milk too early, and it would be a shame to put their little bodies through misery by neglecting to notice signs of sensitivity to milk.

Foods that Could Cause Problems

Food	Problem	Do Not Give to Baby Before Age:
Egg white	Allergy	1
Uncooked honey	Botulism, and possibly death, can occur in babies under a year old	1
Milk	Allergy	1
Wheat	Allergy	10-12 months
Whole berries	Allergy, digestive problems	1½ - 2
Leafy vegetables	Gagging	1½ - 2
Peanut butter (not thinned)	Gagging	2
Popcorn	Choking	2
Whole nuts or seeds	Choking	3
Whole raisins	Choking	2
Whole corn	Gagging	2
Chocolate	Allergy, digestive problems, too much sugar	3 (hold off as long as you can - they don't need it!)
Apple pieces, whole grapes	Choking	1
Candy, cookies	Choking	over age 1 (hold off as long as you can!)
Carrot sticks	Choking	2

 # 7 Coping with Food Allergies

The thousands of additives found in our foods today make it increasingly difficult to pinpoint specific food allergies. It seems the more we learn about allergies, the more complex the subject becomes.

Consider what many doctors and researchers have written about allergies. Food allergies and/or food intolerances:

— can occur at any age
— can appear after eating a food that never caused allergic reactions before
— can cause a reaction anywhere in the body
— cause symptoms to appear only after large amounts have been consumed
— can cause symptons to appear only when foods are eaten during a certain season of the year
— can cause allergic reactions in one child in a family but not a sibling in the same family
— do not cause the same reaction all the time
— often occur in a variety of foods in the same food family

A food allergy occurs when the body has an abnormal reaction after eating a particular food substance; causing one or more distressing symptoms to appear.

A few definitions are needed to help form a better picture of the body's reaction when subjected to an allergic food substance.

An *antigen* is defined as any foreign substance entering the body. Our bodies react to these antigens by producing *antibodies* which help to neutralize the action of the antigen. Food allergies appear when antigens enter the body with a certain food, and the body over-produces antibodies to counteract.

The word *allergy* is derived from the Greek words "allos" meaning "altered" and "ergan" meaning "work" or "action." A food allergy causes an altered action — or intolerance to take place in the body rather than a normal reaction.

Authorities have several theories as to just what causes an allergy. Heredity seems to be the biggest cause of most food allergies. Although it seems specific allergies are not transferred from parent to child, the tendency to react abnormally to various allergens is transferred. More possible causes of food allergy include overeating (some bodies can only cope with a certain amount of an antigen; anything over this amount causes a reaction). Some doctors also believe certain stomach disturbances can cause food allergies.

What are the foods that can cause a food allergy? Any food can cause allergic reactions, but the most common foods are milk, wheat, corn, eggs, citrus, nuts, strawberries and shellfish. Cinnamon, chocolate, and tomatoes also are high on the list. Foods containing artificial additives and dyes are frequent offenders as well.

The following foods are *least* likely to cause problems: rice, oats, barley, peaches, pears, bananas, applesauce, lettuce, carrots, grapes, squash, and sweet potatoes. If one or both parents have a tendency toward allergies, these foods might help to ensure baby gets an allergy-free start when solid foods enter the diet.

Doris Rapp, a well known pediatric allergist, has written several books about children and allergies that would be very helpful to the parent of an allergic child. In her book, *Allergies and Your Child*, Rapp includes a list of food additives frequently causing allergic responses. This list includes:

color additives	thickeners
flavorings	emulsifiers
antioxidants	pesticides
buffers	cod liver oil
preservatives	vitamins
stabilizers	minerals

This presents a rather gloomy situation
finds it necessary to constantly be rea
supermarket.

In their book, *Harmful Food Additives,* Houben and Kropf compiled a specific list of the twenty worst food additives. They are:

BHA and BHT (butylated hydroxyanisole and butylated hydroxytoluene)
caffeine
caramel
carrageenan
EDTA (calcium disodium Ethylenediamine tetraacetate)
hydroxylated lecithin (non-hydroxylated lecithin is acceptable)
lactic acid
maltol dextrin
modified food starch
mono- and diglycerides
monosodium glutamate (MSG)
nitrites, sodium nitrates, sodium
polysorbate 60, 65, 80
propyl gallate
propylene glycol alginate
red dye 40
saccharin
sodium erythorbate
tannin

Symptoms of allergy can range from minor (itching skin or runny nose) to severe (convulsions or even death). Allergic symptoms can appear immediately after eating the offending food, or as long as several days afterward. The most common symptoms of food allergy are:

itching
runny nose
swelling of lips
hives
mouth ulcers
headache
asthma
digestive problems (nausea, vomiting, gas)
irritability
fatigue
behavior problems

As you can see, food allergies are complex and not much fun for anyone involved. The best treatment for food allergy is prevention. If solid foods are introduced slowly, at not too early an age, and baby is given only one new food a week, parents have a better chance of preventing food allergies.

Dr. Lyndon Smith, author of *Foods for Healthy Kids*, and a leading authority on nutrition, recommends: "No solids should be introduced until well after six months of age. It seems boring, but it is safe as it may preclude the development of allergies." Two of his best-selling books, *Feed Your Kids Right* and *Foods for Healthy Kids*, are excellent sources of information for parents interested in maintaining good nutrition for their children.

If your child has a mild reaction to a given food, try waiting a few weeks before offering it again. If the same symptoms appear, eliminate that food from baby's diet. If baby has a violent reaction the first time a food is eaten, *do not* offer the food again. The risk is far too high. In rare instances, death has occured as a result of a severe food allergy. If swelling of the tongue or throat occurs, baby needs immediate medical attention.

Should you suspect allergy, but are not sure which of the variety of foods your baby is eating is the offending one, try eliminating the foods most likely to cause allergy. Your pediatrician can be consulted for further advice on discovering specific food allergies.

The pages that follow include information helpful to a child allergic to milk, eggs, or wheat as well as food diary pages where you can record baby's reactions to new foods.

The Milk-Free Diet

Milk is one of the most common foods causing allergy. Waiting until after baby's first birthday to introduce milk seems to decrease the chance of an allergic response. It does not, however, guarantee none will occur. Look for symptoms of allergy (page 69) when milk is introduced and stop feeding your child milk if symptoms appear.

There are two types of adverse reactions to milk: 1) lactose intolerance and 2) milk allergy. Some people have a *lactose intolerance,* meaning their bodies have difficulty digesting milk. This is because they lack lactase, the enzyme responsible for the digestion of lactose (milk sugar). Children (or adults) with a milk intolerance often can eat yogurt since the fermenting process involved has already broken down the milk sugar. Products such as *Lact-Aid*™, a lactase enzyme powder, also are available to add to whole milk, making it more digestible for the intolerant person.

A *milk allergy* is more severe than a milk intolerance. People with a milk allergy must avoid all milk and milk products. Yogurt or *Lact-Aid*™ would *not* benefit them since they are allergic to the milk itself. Jacqueline Hostage's book, *Living Without Milk,* is an excellent source of information for those needing to plan milk-free diets.

Once it is known or suspected a child is allergic to milk, alternatives need to be found. The knowledge of which foods are necessary to avoid is very important.

Foods to Avoid on a Milk-Free Diet

- All milk beverages: milk, milkshakes, cocoa, chocolate milk, half & half, condensed milk, evaporated milk, skim milk, 1% milk, 2% milk, powdered milk, dried milk, milk solids, and curds and wheys

- Butter, margarine (check labels: some margarines are milk-free)

- Cream, sour cream, whipping cream, buttermilk

- Cheeses, (including cottage cheese)

- Yogurt

- Custards

- Breads made with milk or milk products, biscuits, muffins, pancakes, waffles, crackers

- Cookies, cakes, ice cream, puddings, doughnuts, pies, and desserts made with milk or milk products

- Creamed soups, vegetables, sauces, gravies

- Canned or dehydrated soups made with milk or milk products

- Milk chocolate

- Mashed potatoes

- Salad dressings containing milk or milk products

- Casein, sodium caseinate, and lactalbumin (proteins in milk). Watch closely for these when reading labels!

Once you know or suspect your child is allergic to milk, consult immediately with your child's doctor. The pediatrician can provide specific nutritional information and guidance in dealing with milk allergies.

When avoiding milk in the diet, the following liquids can be substituted: soymilks, soy formulas, non-dairy creamers (avoid brands containing sodium caseinate), coconut milk (avoid brands containing sodium caseinate), and nut milks.

Egg Free Diet

Many childhood vaccines (such as polio, measles, and influenza) are grown on eggs — causing allergic symptoms to appear in people who are extremely sensitive to eggs. Consult your child's doctor if you even suspect egg allergy in your child. Some people who are allergic to eggs also are allergic to chicken.

The "egg-replacers" found in the supermarket are not always egg-free. These are made for people concerned with low cholesteral diet, so read the labels!!

There seem to be few good substitutes for eggs, but a little bit of tofu (about 2 ounces) sometimes can work quite well in recipes. Experimentation and imagination will be helpful here.

Eggs provide excellent nutrients, including protein, fat, and iron, but are not an essential part of a diet. Watching out for foods containing eggs can be tricky, so label reading is a must.

Foods to Avoid on an Egg-Free Diet

Beverages made with eggs; egg nog, malted shakes, root beer

Noodles or pasta made with eggs

Desserts made with eggs; ice cream, cookies, cakes, cream pies, meringue pies, custards, sherbets, candies

Hollandaise sauce, tartar sauce

Bread products made with eggs, breaded foods

Pancakes, waffles, French toast

Doughnuts

Pretzels

Dried or powdered eggs

Egg whites or yolks

Egg white solids

Egg albumin

Mayonnaise, salad dressings containing eggs

Meatloaf or meat dishes containing eggs

Cake mixes or other prepared mixes containing egg products or egg ingredients

Egg dishes (scrambled, baked, fried, or boiled eggs, omelets, quiches, souffles)

Poultry or fish dishes containing eggs

Baking powders that contain egg white or albumen

Coffee or wine if clarified with egg white or shell

Soups, any soup containing egg products or ingredients

Wheat-Free Diet

Wheat is another food that frequently causes allergic reactions. Rice, barley, and oats usually are the first cereals offered baby in order to avoid possible allergic reactions.

Foods to Avoid on a Wheat-Free Diet

Flour: white, whole-wheat, enriched, unbleached, graham

Wheat bran or wheat germ

Wheat gluten or wheat starch

Malt, malted milk

Farina

Monosodium glutamate

Breads, bisquits, muffins, rolls, crackers, pretzels

Doughnuts

Pancakes, waffles

Bread crumbs

Pasta

Desserts made with flour (pies, cakes, cookies, candies)

Coffee substitutes

Ovaltine

Most beers, gin, and whiskey

Gravy, sauces, tamari sauce

Processed cheese (some contain wheat stabilizers)

Some meat products (canned meats, hotdogs, sausage, meatloaf, lunch meats)

Good substitutions for 1 cup wheat flour

1¼ cup rye flour

1⅓ cup oat flour

⅝ cup potato starch (flour)

⅞ cup rice flour

¾ cup barley flour

¾ cup corn meal

Experimentation and perseverence will be necessary when substituting other flours for wheat flour, since some recipes work better than others when substituting different types of flours.

Baby's Food Diary

Food introduced	Baby's age	Today's date	Liked	Disliked	Adverse Reaction	Time food was given	Time of reaction

Baby's Food Diary

Food introduced	Baby's age	Today's date	Liked	Disliked	Adverse Reaction	Time food was given	Time of reaction

8 Beginner Recipes (4-6 months)

The beginners recipes are for babies four to six months, who are starting to eat solid foods. Early feeding need not be elaborate and baby doesn't need a wide variety of choices. This section contains recipes for cereals and fruits. A slow introduction of each new food is recommended (see Chapter 6, "How to Feed Your Baby"). Three time-saving ideas are included in this section:

- making large batches of fruits to purée and freeze in ice cube trays
- grinding grains ahead of time and storing in jars for daily use, and
- the use of the pressure cooker.

Here are a few more ideas for those first days of introducing solid foods to your baby:

1. Choose a non-fussy time to begin feeding solid food. Between bottles or nursings is usually a good time.
2. Start with small spoonfuls of each new food. Feed gently and in a relaxed manner.
3. Never save foods that baby doesn't finish. The serving spoon mixes saliva into the remaining food and this saliva breaks down the food causing a loss in nutritional value and freshness.
4. Take time to enjoy baby's meal times. Household chores will always be there but your infant baby won't stay little very long. (Honest!) Have fun!

Introduce (4-6 months):

Fruits
  banana
  avocado
  papaya
  pears
  apples
  plums
  apricots

Grains
  rice
  barley
  oats
  millet

> Offer one new food a week, all foods in puréed form. One meal a day can be given for the first weeks of feeding solids. Gradually increase to two meals.

Sample Menu
For Beginners

Breakfast: Rice cereal

Dinner: Apple purée

Plus: Breast milk or formula at least 3 times a day

Avocado-ado!

2-3 tablespoons ripe avocado, peeled

Mash with fork or blend through a baby food grinder. You can add breast milk or formula for the first few feedings.

A few words about the avocado: If you have never eaten an avocado — please don't toss this recipe aside! Avocados are a great first food for baby. They are soft, bland, and high in Vitamin A. Don't assume your baby won't like avocados if you have never tasted them — like I almost did! (Although this is primarily a baby food cookbook, I must mention this: a great way for grown-ups to taste avocados is by putting little chunks in a salad, or eating them with a bit of lemon juice and oil dressing, or made into guacamole.) When choosing an avocado, purchase one that is soft (not mushy) to the touch — or buy a firm avocado and let it sit out a few days until it gets soft.

Banana-ana!

½ ripe banana, peeled

Mash with fork or put through a baby food grinder. Add a bit of breast milk or formula to thin for initial feedings.

Avocado Banana Cream
(affectionately called "That Green Stuff")

½ banana
¼ - ½ small avocado

Blend thoroughly in a baby food grinder.

Fruit Purée

Large quantity of fruit (babies like apples, pears, peaches, plums, apricots) — washed, peeled, and chopped

Add ¼ cup boiling water to each cup of fruit.

Simmer until tender. Blend everything (include water) in blender. Serve warm or cool. Freeze remainder in ice cube trays. Thaw 2 or 3 cubes when needed. Fruit can be served warm or at room temperature.

Pressure cooker method: Place washed, pared fruit (remove seeds) on rack and add 1 cup water. Do not fill pressure cooker over two-thirds full. Cook according to the timetable below, allowing pressure regulator to rock slowly during cooking. Cool cooker under faucet of cool running water until pressure drops to normal. Purée in blender or food processor and freeze in ice cube trays.

Fruit	Cooking Time
apples (whole)	7 minutes
apricots (whole)	2 minutes
peaches (whole)	5 minutes
pears (whole)	6-8 minutes
plums	2 minutes

Dried Fruit Purée

*1 cup dried fruit (apricots, papayas, peaches, pears,
    apples)*
Water to cover

Place in covered container and soak overnight in refrigerator.
Pour into the blender the next day and purée. Serve and
refrigerate remainder no more than three (3) days.

Dried Fruit Purée
(Quick Method)

Put fruit and water in saucepan, cover, and simmer until soft
(10-20 minutes). Purée in blender. Great mixed with yogurt
or cereal!

Pressure cooker method: Place dried fruit on rack and add
water to cover. Do not fill pressure cooker over two-thirds
full. Cook according to time table below, allowing pressure
regulator to rock slowly during cooking. Cool cooker under
faucet of cool running water until pressure drops to normal.
Purée in blender or food processor and freeze in ice cube trays.

Dried Fruit	Cooking Time
apples	6-8 minutes
apricots	6-8 minutes
figs	20-25 minutes
papaya	8-10 minutes
peaches	6-8 minutes
pears	6-8 minutes
prunes	6-8 minutes

Note: Cooking time varies depending on fruit size, so use the
longer cooking time for the larger size fruits.

Rice Cereal

¼ cup rice powder (brown rice ground in blender*)
1 cup breast milk, water, or formula

In saucepan, bring liquid to boil. Sprinkle in rice powder, stirring constantly. Simmer covered for 10 minutes. This is good with puréed fruit. Serve warm.

*To grind large amounts of rice, barley, millet or oatmeal: place ¾ cup of grain in the blender and whiz at high speed 20-30 seconds. Store in sterile, glass jars. (Oatmeal can be ground in a food processor but the other grains do better in the blender.)

Barley Cereal

¼ cup ground barley (ground in the blender)
1 cup breast milk, water, or formula

Bring liquid to a boil. Add barley and simmer 10 minutes. Serve warm. (Add more liquid for thinner consistency.)

Oatmeal

¼ cup ground oats (Don't use the instant kind — just
grind regular oatmeal in blender or food processor)
¾ cup water

Bring water to boil. Add oats, cover, simmer 5 minutes. Serve warm with added breast milk or formula, apple juice, or puréed fruit.

Millet Cereal

3 tablespoons ground millet
1 cup breast milk, water, or formula

Bring liquid to a boil. Add millet stirring constantly for a minute. Simmer for 10 minutes. Serve warm.

Rice, Oat or Barley Cereal
(Method 2)

Cook grains (without grinding them first) by normal method omitting salt (see page 00 for cooking time). After grains are cooked, blend in the blender or food processor until smooth. This is an easy way to cook cereal when other children or family members are eating the same foods together.

Combination Cereal

1 tablespoon ground oats
1 tablespoon ground rice
1 tablespoon ground barley
¾ - 1 cup water

Bring water to a boil. Add grains and stir with wire whip. Cover and simmer 10 minutes. Serve warm.

9 Intermediate Recipes (7-9 months)

Intermediates (7 to 9 month olds) are getting the knack of being spoon fed. Most of them are ready to venture into the world of vegetables and different cereal combinations. Introduced in this section are recipes for vegetables, cereal, yogurt, smoothies, tofu, and various lunch ideas. Baby should now be eating two meals a day plus juice or a smoothie "snack". Look for possible milk allergy after introducing yogurt and other milk and cheese products.

Introduce: (7-9 months)

Mild vegetables
    carrots
    green beans
    peas
    zucchini
    squash

Yogurt

Egg yolk (cooked)

Beverages
    mild juices — apple,
    apricot, papaya
    smoothies

Tofu

Cheese

> Continue introducing one new food per week. Begin combining fruits with cereals. Juice or smoothie can be given for a snack. Bagel, biscuits, or bread can be given to help with teething. Watch closely for choking or gagging. Gradually increase to three meals a day. Continue to purée most foods but begin to offer thicker, lumpier foods. Watch for possible food allergy.

Sample Menu
For Intermediates

Breakfast: Oatmeal plus apple juice

Lunch: Tofu - banana whip or smoothie

Dinner: Baby vegetable purée

Plus: Breast milk or formula 2-3 times a day

Baby Vegetable Purée

*Large quantity of fresh vegetables (choose from carrots,
green beans, peas, zucchini, etc.)
Add at least two inches of water in saucepan*

Cover and cook until tender. Blend; serve warm. Freeze remainder in ice cube trays.

Pressure Cooker Method: Using a pressure cooker to cook vegetables saves most of the valuable vitamins and minerals that can escape during regular cooking. Clean and chop vegetables; add ½ to 1 cup water; and cook according to pressure cooker directions. Don't forget to include the cooking water when you purée vegetables in the blender. This method allows you to prepare a large quantity at a time.

Steamed Vegetables

*2 cups chopped fresh vegetables
1½ cups water*

In a saucepan, bring water to a boil under the steam basket. Place vegetables in basket and check water level to be sure water is not touching vegetables. Cover and steam until tender (usually about 10 minutes, if vegetables are cut small.) Blend; serve. Freeze remainder.

Homemade Yogurt

4 cups milk

¼ cup non-fat dry milk (optional but good to add when using low-fat or skim milk because it makes a thicker, creamier yogurt)

2 tablespoons unpasteurized, plain yogurt or 1 package dried yogurt culture (purchase at natural foods store)

In a small bowl, add non-fat milk to 1 cup milk and stir until dissolved. Pour into saucepan and add remaining 3 cups of milk. Mix well. Heat over low heat until milk starts to bubble around the edges of the saucepan. Remove from heat and cool to 105°F. to 115°F. (Milk should feel very warm if tested on the wrist). Remove 1 cup warm milk and place in a small bowl. Stir in yogurt or yogurt culture until dissolved. Add to remaining milk and stir again. Pour into individual containers of a yogurt maker or into sterile glass jars. Cover. Incubate in yogurt maker for 6 to 10 hours or use one of the following methods:

1. Place jars of yogurt on a heating pad and wrap tightly with towels or a small blanket.
2. Place in electric oven set on lowest possible temperature.
3. Place a hot-water bottle at the bottom of a large cooking pot. Place yogurt on top and cover tightly. Wrap pan in towels.
4. Place in metal cooking pan and set close to wood stove.

(A constant temperature of 110°F. is ideal during incubation period.)

Helpful Yogurt Making Tips

- If using homemade yogurt, be sure it is no more than five days old.

- Do not use yogurt that contains stabilizers — read labels closely.

- Be gentle with yogurt. Fold gently when adding yogurt to other ingredients.

- Do not add fruit to yogurt during cooking time. Dried fruits should be added right before yogurt is put in the refrigerator. Other fruits should be added at serving time.

- Yogurt tastes best if used within 2 weeks. After that time, yogurt is best used in cooking since it develops a sharper flavor.

Fruit Yogurt*

3 tablespoons plain yogurt (not low fat)
2 tablespoons puréed fruit (apples, peaches, bananas,
*   apricots)*

Mix together and serve. Most babies will love yogurt, even if their parents don't!

Note: The higher fat content in whole milk makes it easier to digest in infants than yogurt made with skim milk. If baby is overweight, the switch to low fat yogurt can be made at age one.

*No berries until age two (2).

Smoothies

½ cup fruit (peaches, papayas, bananas, apricots)
½ cup milk (breast milk or formula before age one (1))
¼ cup whole milk yogurt (plain)*
¼ teaspoon vanilla extract
1 teaspoon blackstrap molasses (or honey after age one
*   (1)*

Blend in blender. Serves baby plus one!

*Although yogurt is easily digested and usually well tolerated by infants, a child with an allergy to milk will have an allergic reaction to yogurt because it is a milk product. If any reaction occurs, stop all milk products and check with the pediatrician for suggestions on when to re-introduce milk into baby's diet.

Simple Banana Smoothie

½ cup plain yogurt
½ banana
¼ teaspoon blackstrap molasses (or honey after age 1)
Dash of vanilla

Combine all ingredients in a blender. Serve at once. One serving. (Double the recipe if you want enough for a thirsty toddler or thirsty grown-up!)

Oatmeal Plus

1¼ *cup water*
¼ *cup oatmeal (rice or barley can also be used)*
¼ *cup chopped dates, raisins, peaches or apricots*
1 *teaspoon finely ground almonds (optional)*

Bring water to a boil. Add remaining ingredients. Cover and simmer for 5 minutes. Purée in grinder or blender. Serve warm.

Tofu-Banana Whip
(Often called "toe-food" around our house)

½ *banana*
1 *tablespoon tofu*

Mash with fork and blend until smooth. Great on rice cakes or on peanut butter bread!

Note: *Tofu* is made from soybeans in a way similar to the way cheese is made from milk. It looks like a cube of ricotta cheese, but it really has a very bland taste. It is full of protein, low in calories, and for these reasons it is a great "extender" food. Store tofu in the refrigerator and keep it covered with water. If the water is changed daily (or almost every day!) tofu will last up to 10 days. If it doesn't smell fresh — don't use it. Draining tofu on a paper towel helps remove excess water before combining it with other ingredients. Tofu is usually found in the produce department at your grocery store or in natural foods stores. Check the date to ensure freshness.

Baby Rice Pudding

½ cup brown rice
2 cups milk (formula, breast milk, or water before age 1)
1 egg yolk (or whole egg after age 1)
¼ teaspoon vanilla extract
1 teaspoon blackstrap molasses

Rinse rice. Combine all ingredients in saucepan. Bring to a boil; then simmer 1 hour. (Check to see if more liquid needs to be added.) Let cool. Put through blender or baby food grinder. Good served warm or cold.

Cottage Cheese Lunch*

Combine 3 tablespoons of cottage cheese with one of the following:

3 tablespoons applesauce or,
3 tablespoons puréed fruit or 2 thawed fruit purée cubes (apples, peaches, pears, apricots) or, ¼ small, ripe avacodo, mashed

Blend in baby food grinder and serve.

*Be on the look out for milk allergy after introducing cottage cheese.

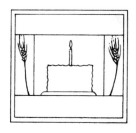

10 Advanced Recipes (10-12 months)

"Advanced" babies are getting more lovable by the minute. These 10, 11, and 12 month olds are sprouting a few teeth (some babies' first teeth arrive later so don't panic if you have a toothless babe now) and good strong gums. These babies begin to see a lot of options available on their daily menus. Grains, beans, egg yolks, and a wider variety of vegetables are available for them. Begin watching for wheat and egg allergy and be careful not to overfeed! Remember to let baby use teeth and gums to chew or mix the food.

Introduce: (10-12 months)

Legumes
    cooked dry beans
        and peas
    thinned peanut
        butter and nut
        butters
    ground sprouts

Grains
    bulghur
    wheat

Vegetables
    stronger vegetables,
    broccoli, cabbage,
    cauliflower

Cheese
    small cheese cubes
    shredded, melted cheese

> Meals can begin to be in less puréed form but avoid large chunks of food. Finger foods can be offered. Continue to watch for reactions or allergies to any new (or old) food. Advanced babies can have three meals a day plus juices and healthy snacks.

Sample Menu
for Advanced Babies

Breakfast: Whole wheat pancakes with fruit purée, apple or papaya juice

Lunch: Bunny yogurt or carrot-zucchini shred

Snack: Rice cake with a bit of thinned peanut butter or fruit or cheese pieces

Dinner: Rice 'n Beans and mashed carrot or soft carrot pieces or
Garden Casserole and whole wheat bread or crackers

Plus: Breast milk or formula 3 times a day

Bulghur & Vegetables

¾ cup boiling water
⅓ cup bulghur
2 tablespoons grated zucchini
2 tablespoons grated carrot
1 tablespoon shredded cheese (optional)

Bring water to a boil in a saucepan. Sprinkle bulghur, zucchini, and carrot into water and stir briefly. Cover and let stand for 5 minutes. Put through baby food grinder. Sprinkle with cheese and stir. Serve warm.

Lentils & Rice

¼ cup cooked lentils
¾ cup cooked brown rice

Blend together and purée with a little cooking water from lentils. Serve warm. This makes 2 servings.

Rice 'n Beans

3 tablespoons cooked brown rice
1 tablespoon cooked beans (pinto, black, or other beans)
2 tablespoons cooking water (from beans)
1 tablespoon shredded cheese

Mix all ingredients. Heat in a saucepan until cheese melts. Blend through grinder or serve as is, if baby is receptive to lumpy food. This is a nice main meal protein dish.

Broccoli & Rice

¼ cup chopped, cooked broccoli
½ cup cooked brown rice or bulghur
¼ cup cooked barley
¼ cup cooking water from broccoli
2 tablespoons grated cheese

Combine first four ingredients and heat in a saucepan (no longer than 2-3 minutes, since broccoli and grains are already cooked.) Put through a baby food grinder and top with cheese or serve as is if your baby can chew lumpy food. Enough for 2 servings (one for dinner and one reheated the next day for lunch).

Carrot 'n Bean Soup

1 carrot, chopped
1 cup green beans, chopped
2 cups water

Place ingredients in a saucepan. Cover. Simmer until tender (about 30 minutes — depending on size of cut vegetables). Blend carrots, beans, and cooking water together in blender. Serve warm. For a large batch, just increase all ingredients proportionally. Freeze in ice cube trays.

Pressure cooker method: Decrease water to 3 cups. Cook 8 minutes after pressure regulator begins to rock.

Bean Preparation

Use 1 Cup of	Soaking Required	Water	Cooking Time	Approx. Yield
Baby limas: use in casseroles, side dishes	Yes	2 cups	1½ hr.	1¾ cup
Black-eyed peas: use in main dishes, southern cookery	Yes	3 cups	1 hr.	2 cups
Black (turtle) beans: use in soups, Mexican dishes	Yes	4 cups	1½ hr.	2 cups
Garbanzos (chick peas): use in soups, salads, dips	Yes	4 cups	2½-3 hrs.	2 cups
Great Northern beans: use in baked beans, soups, main dishes	Yes	3½ cups	2 hrs.	2 cups
Kidney Beans: use in chili, Mexican dishes	Yes	3 cups	1½-2 hrs.	2 cups
Lentils: use in soups, casseroles	No	3 cups	1 hr.	2¼ cups
Lima beans: use in side dishes, casseroles	Yes	2 cups	1½-2 hrs.	1¼ cups
Navy beans (white beans): use in main dishes	Yes	3 cups	2½-3 hrs.	2 cups

Use 1 Cup of	Soaking Required	Water	Cooking Time	Approx. Yield
Pea beans: use in baked beans	Yes	3 cups	2 hrs.	2 cups
Pinto beans: use in refried beans, chili, main dishes, Mexican dishes	Yes	3 cups	2 hrs.	2 cups
Soy beans: use in soups, main dishes, casseroles	Yes	4 cups	3 hrs.	2 cups
Split peas: use in soups, main dishes	No	3 cups	1 hr.	2¼ cups

How to Cook Beans

Rinse beans well under cold running water. Discard any cracked beans or small rocks while rinsing. Soak beans overnight. (Soybeans must be soaked in the refrigerator but all other beans can remain at room temperature.) Place beans and water in a saucepan (use soaking water and add more water if necessary). Cover loosely and simmer for approximate amount of time specified above. Do not add salt or oil during cooking. A clove of garlic, or small onion may be added if desired. Test beans for tenderness and adjust cooking time accordingly since the extact time varies.

Quick soak method: Forget to soak the beans the night before? Bring water and beans to a boil. Simmer 2-3 minutes, then cover and let soak for 2 hours. Cook beans according to above directions.

Cooking Grains

Use 1 Cup of:	Water	Cooking Time	Approx. Yield
Barley	3 cups	1 hr. 15 min.	3½ cups
Brown rice	2 cups	1 hr.	3 cups
Buckwheat groats (Kasha)	2 cups	15 min.	2½ cups
Bulghur wheat	2 cups	15-20 mins.	2½ cups
Cracked wheat	2 cups	25 mins.	2⅓ cups
Corn meal	4 cups	25 mins.	3 cups
Millet	3 cups	45 mins.	3½ cups
Oatmeal	2 cups	15 mins.	2 cups
Whole wheat berries	3 cups	1 hr.	2¼ cups
Wild rice	3 cups	1 hr.	4 cups

How to Cook Grains

Bring water to boil in a saucepan. Slowly sprinkle grain into boiling water. Cover and simmer over low heat for the amount of time specified in above chart. Do not add salt during cooking time.

Rice-Squash

1 tablespoon brown rice
1 tablespoon squash (acorn, green, yellow)

Cook rice until almost tender, about 40 minutes. Add squash pieces and complete cooking. Blend in blender or grinder. (Good to have when rice is included in the family menu.)

Colorful Barley

1 *cup water*
1 *tablespoon uncooked barley, ground fine*
1 *tablespoon peas*
½ *carrot, grated*

Bring water to a boil. Sprinkle barley powder in with wire whip. Add peas and carrots. Simmer 15 minutes or until vegetables are tender. Serve warm.

Garden Casserole

Broccoli
Cauliflower
Carrots
Potatoes
Cheese

Chop vegetables and steam until tender. Top with a bit of baby's favorite cheese and serve warm.

Lentil Cheeseburgers

½ *cup lentils*
1 *egg yolk*
Dash of thyme (optional)
1 *tablespoon whole wheat bread crumbs or wheat germ*
Monterey Jack or Swiss cheese

Cook lentils until soft so they mash easily with a fork, about 1 hour. Drain any excess water and save for soup stock. When lentils are cool, add egg yolk, bread crumbs, and thyme. Shape into patties. Bake 15 minutes at 350°F. Add cheese slices and return to oven until cheese melts. Serve warm. (Be sure cheese has cooled to avoid a bad burn!)

Whole Wheat Pancakes

⅓ to ½ cup whole-wheat flour
1 teaspoon baking powder
1½ teaspoon honey
½ cup milk
1 egg yolk
1½ teaspoon oil

Combine dry ingredients. Combine liquid ingredients. Stir into dry ingredients only till moistened. Cook in lightly oiled skillet. Enough for 2 servings. Refrigerate leftover pancakes for next day. Reheat briefly in dry skillet — just till warm. Serve with yogurt and fruit.

Note: Pancakes are great for any meal, but lunchtime pancakes are usually a favorite with babies and toddlers. Babies enjoy picking up bite-size pieces and feeding themselves.

Zucchini Pancakes

1 zucchini, grated
1 egg yolk (add whole egg after age 1)
½ cup whole-wheat flour
2 tablespoons mashed tofu (optional)
⅓ cup milk
¼ teaspoon baking powder

Mix all ingredients just until moistened. Cook in oiled skillet until lightly browned — just like regular pancakes. This is a great finger-food favorite! Wrap leftovers in foil and reheat the next day. These also freeze well. Good fingerfood!

Potato Pancakes

2 potatoes, shredded fine or processed in food processor
1 egg yolk (whole egg after age 1)
2 tablespoons flour

Combine all ingredients in mixing bowl. Pour batter by large spoonfuls onto oiled skillet. Flip when edges turn lightly brown. Serve at room temperature. This is another good finger food!

Cottage Cheese Pancakes

½ *cup cottage cheese*
1 *egg yolk*
½ *cup whole-wheat flour*
⅓ *cup milk*
¼ *teaspoon baking powder*

Mix all ingredients. Cook in lightly oiled skillet until lightly browned on both sides. Good topped with applesauce.

Meredith's Omelet

1 *egg yolk (whole egg after age 1)*
1 *tablespoon milk*
1 *teaspoon butter*
2 *tablespoons grated cheese*

Combine egg and milk and beat with a fork. Melt butter over low heat in a 7-inch skillet. Pour egg mixture into skillet and tilt skillet often so egg mixture becomes firm. Lift batter in some places with a fork so egg mixture touches hot skillet. When egg is cooked, add cheese and fold omelet in half. Keep in the skillet for 15 or more seconds and serve warm. Be careful cheese has cooled enough for baby to eat safely. Green pepper, zucchini, or shredded cooked potato can also be added for variation.

Note: Be sure egg mixture is entirely cooked. Also — be on the lookout for allergic reactions to eggs!

Apple Delight

½ *apple, pared*
½ *banana*
½ *carrot*
¼ *cup apple juice*

Whiz in blender until smooth. This can be spoon fed to baby or served in a cup with larger holes in the lid. A wonderful lunch served with a muffin or toast!

Sprout Growing

Seeds*	Sprouting Time	Especially Good in:
Alfalfa	4 to 5 days	Salads, sandwiches, vegetables
Garbanzo beans	3 days	Salads, sandwiches, soups, vegetables
Lentils	3 to 4 days	Salads, soups, vegetables
Mung beans	3 to 4 days	Salads, soups, Chinese dishes
Radish	3 to 4 days	Salads, sandwiches
Sunflower	2 days	Salads, sandwiches, breads, vegetables
Soybeans**	3 days	Soups, vegetables
Wheat berries	2 days	Breads, vegetables

*Be sure to purchase untreated seeds meant for eating and cooking — *not* planting. Seeds for planting are chemically treated and should not be sprouted.

**Soybean sprouts must *not* be eaten raw since they contain a protein-inhibiting enzyme. Steam soybean sprouts at least 5 minutes before eating.

Equipment needed for sprouting:
Wide mouth quart jar, sterile
2 layers of cheesecloth, nylon net, or a wash cloth
Rubber band or ring of a Mason jar

How to Sprout

1. Rinse seeds or beans and sort out any that are cracked, discolored, or damaged. Soak 1 tablespoon seeds or ⅓ cup beans in a clean jar filled with one quart of warm water overnight.
2. In the morning, secure cheesecloth over the jar opening with a rubber band.
3. Pour out rinse water through the cheesecloth and rinse seeds thoroughly with warm water. (Fill jar with water and pour out — repeat several times.)

4. Turn jar upside down so water drains out. Store sprouts on the kitchen counter or in a cupboard (sprouts will grow in dark or light area, however mung bean sprouts grow best in the dark). Keep jar out of direct sunlight. Be sure to drain well so seeds do not get moldy.
5. Gently rinse sprouts 2 or 3 times a day. Drain well after each rinsing.
6. When seeds are ready (check "Sprout Growing" Chart for time) rinse in cold water. Drain well and store in refrigerator up to 1 week. The sooner the sprouts are used the higher the nutritional value.
7. Bring alfalfa and other leafy sprouts out of the darkness the last day into indirect sunlight. The light provides a pretty green leaf and added chlorophyll.
8. Eat and enjoy the sprouts! They can be used in salads, sandwiches, breads, or vegetable dishes. Children can easily grow sprouts with a little help from a grown-up. Everyone enjoys watching them grow — and they taste so good!

Carrot Salad

2 tablespoons finely grated carrot
2 tablespoons finely grated apples
7-8 pre-soaked raisins
1 tablespoon yogurt

Soak raisins in ½ cup water at breakfast so they'll be soft by lunchtime. Be sure to blend raisins thoroughly in a blender or food grinder at this age. Wait until age 2 to introduce whole raisins since they can cause choking. Blend through a baby food grinder and serve.

Vegetable Lunch

2 tablespoons finely grated zucchini
1 tablespoon alfalfa sprouts (optional)
2 tablespoons finely grated carrots

Whiz in blender. Add yogurt for a different treat!
A word about sprouts: Sprouts are springing up (oh no) in the produce section of most grocery stores. These are full of protein and a great addition to salads as well as other foods. They are easy to grow in your own kitchen.

Bunny Yogurt

3 tablespoons finely grated carrot
3 tablespoons yogurt

Blend and serve.

Bunny Yogurt II

2 tablespoons grated carrot
2 tablespoons grated raw broccoli
2-3 tablespoons plain yogurt

Blend through a baby food grinder and serve. This makes a nice lunch served with whole wheat toast and juice.

Carrot-Zucchini Shred

½ carrot, grated
½ zucchini, grated

Steam carrot and zucchini in steamer 10 minutes or until soft. Blend through grinder with 2 tablespoons cooking water or serve as is to older baby.

This can also be served raw after whizzing through processor or blender.

Baked Sweet Potatoes

Bake sweet potato in 350°F oven for 1 hour. Scoop out potatoes, mash with a fork. Serve warm. Use a bit of apple juice or other liquid to cool potato.

Potatoes Deluxe

½ baked potato, shredded
¼ cup cottage cheese
1-2 tablespoons formula or breast milk

Combine potatoes and cottage cheese. Add liquid to thin mixture so it's suitable for baby. Serve. This is a great way to use leftover baked potatoes.

Appled Sweet Potatoes

1 medium sweet potato, baked
½ cup apple, puréed, or applesauce
¼ cup breast milk, formula, or apple juice

Skin and mash baked sweet potato. Add liquid and apple sauce. Mix gently. Place in lightly buttered baking dish. Cover. Bake 30 minutes at 350°F. Makes 2-3 servings. Leftovers can be reheated in a small saucepan the next day.

This recipe takes a little more time than usual, but it's a real favorite! This is a good recipe to plan when your family menu includes sweet potatoes.

Baked Acorn Squash

1 acorn squash
1 tablespoon butter
1 tablespoon honey

Slice acorn squash in half. Scoop out inside seeds. Add butter and honey to the center of each half. Bake on foil-lined pan at 350°F. for 45 minutes or until tender. Greatly appreciated by adults, too!

Peanut Butter Delight

½ banana, mashed
2 tablespoons peanut butter
2 tablespoons tofu

Blend in baby food grinder and serve. Thin with milk, if necessary. This is good on rice cakes or whole wheat toast too!

Elizabeth's Peanut Butter Pudding

2 tablespoons peanut butter
2 tablespoons applesauce or puréed apple
½ banana

Blend through a baby food grinder or mash with fork. Serve at room temperature.

Baby's 1st Birthday Cake

1 cup honey
4 tablespoons brown sugar
2 cups whole-wheat flour (or 1 cup unbleached and 1
    cup whole wheat)
½ teaspoon salt
2 teaspoons cinnamon
2 teaspoons soda
4 large eggs
1½ cups oil
2 cups grated carrots

Grease a 9"x13" pan. Mix all dry ingredients and sift. Beat eggs, oil, and honey. Add to dry ingredients and mix. Add carrots. Bake 30 minutes at 350°F. Top with cream cheese icing.

Cream Cheese Icing

2 8-ounce packages cream cheese
¼ cup cooked honey
1 teaspoon vanilla
1 tablespoon butter (optional)

Have cream cheese at room temperature. Blend all ingredients.
Note: Cream cheese is high in saturated fat and not high on the list of cheeses that offer quality nutrients. It should be used sparingly or replaced with kefir cheese, yogurt cheese, Neufchatel cheese, tofu, or low fat cottage cheese whipped in the blender.

Gingerbread Shortcake

½ cup butter
1 cup molasses
1 cup sour cream or yogurt
2⅓ cups flour
dash salt
¾ teaspoon baking soda
1 teaspoon ground cinnamon
1 teaspoon ground ginger
¼ teaspoon ground cloves
2 bananas, sliced
whipping cream

Combine butter and molasses in a small saucepan and bring to a boil. Add sour cream or yogurt. Sift all dry ingredients and add to molasses mixture and stir. Pour into square baking pan and bake at 350°F for 40 minutes. At serving time, remove from pan and cut into squares. Split squares into 2 layers and place sliced bananas between the layers. Top with whipped cream. Especially good served warm on a special occassion.

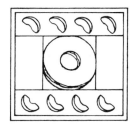 # 11 Toddle Food Recipes (1-3 years)

As baby begins to toddle about (at around age one), then run about (here comes the terrific twos and threes!), they need especially nutritious foods available when they stop for a quick moment to grab a bite to eat. And often "a bite to eat" is all they'll settle for at any given moment. They're too busy exploring their fascinating world! It seems at times as if two-year-olds live on air. Other times they'll attempt to clean out your refrigerator (with or without your help . . .).

Nutritious finger foods are essential for toddlers. Here are a few foods they can grab on the run: cheese cubes, rice cakes, puffed cereals, crackers, fruit pieces, muffins, bagels, toast, and fresh vegetables. When "toddlers" feel like a real "meal" — they can be given many good foods from the grown-up's menu. Various beverages and frozen "popsicles" can provide essential vitamins and minerals between "meals".

Along with a variety of recipes especially enjoyed by toddlers, there are two recipes to help mom or dad out on a cold or rainy day. "Laura's Play Dough" and "Kid's Stuff" are two *non-edible* recipes to help make the day more enjoyable for all. Have fun during this wonderful, growing, and toddling time!

Introduce (1-3 years):

Nutritious finger foods, new vegetables, fruits, or grains

Three meals a day plus a snack or two can be given. Foods are lumpier and rarely need to be blended in the baby food grinder. Be sure all snacks are healthy ones since Toddlers do not always stop to eat a complete meal. Continue to watch closely for signs of allergy.

[105]

Sample menu
for Toddlers

Breakfast: Granola or Familia with milk or yogurt
orange juice

Snack: fruit pieces

Lunch: Cottage Cheese Delight, Oatmeal Muffin,
and Banana Smoothie

Snack: Molly's Juice Bar or vegetable pieces

Dinner: Whole-Wheat Pizza and salad or Falafel
Burgers in pita bread, green beans

Plus: 2-3 servings of milk or yogurt

Sunny Smoothie

¼ *cup yogurt or milk*
¼ *cup orange juice*
½ *banana*
¼ *teaspoon blackstrap molasses or 1 teaspoon honey*
Dash of vanilla

Blend well in blender. Serve at once. A great dessert treat!

Carob Milk

1 cup milk
*1 tablespoon melted carob chips or 1 tablespoon carob
powder*
2 teaspoons honey

Blend in blender and drink. Serves 1.

Carob Delight

1 *cup milk*
2 *teaspoons carob powder*
2 *teaspoons honey*
1 *teaspoon non-instant milk*
¼ *teaspoon lecithin granuals (optional)*

Blend all ingredients in the blender. Drink! Serves 1.

Brown Monkey Shake

1 *cup milk*
1 *banana*
2 *teaspoons carob powder*
1 *teaspoon honey*
1 *teaspoon non-instant dry milk*

Blend in blender. Serves 1.

Cranberry Punch

48 *ounces cranberry juice*
1 *large can (46-ounce) unsweetened pineapple juice*
1½ *quarts (48-ounce) orange juice*
Juice from one lemon

Mix all juices together. Chill and serve over ice. This recipe makes enough to have for a few days! A wonderful thirst-quenching drink. (It's fun to make punch ice cubes from this recipe too. Add the colorful cubes to the punch or a glass of orange juice!)

Granola

4 cups old-fashioned oats
1 cup sesame seeds
1 cup sunflower seeds
1 cup wheat germ (raw)
1 cup unsweetened coconut
½ cup non-instant dry milk
½ cup honey
½ cup safflower oil
1 teaspoon vanilla
½ cup almonds, chopped
½ cup raisins

Toss dry ingredients (except raisins and almonds) in a large bowl. Mix honey, oil, and vanilla together and pour over oatmeal mixture. Stir. Pour onto baking sheet and bake in 300°F. oven for 30 minutes, stirring several times. Add almonds and raisins during the last 5 minutes. Remove from oven and cool completely before storing in a large glass jar with a tight fitting lid.

Corn Meal Cereal

¼ cup yellow corn meal
1 cup water

Using a double broiler, bring water to a boil. Slowly sprinkle corn meal into water, stirring constantly with a wire whip or wooden spoon. Simmer 15 minutes. Let stand 15 minutes. Add a dot of butter, dash of honey, and thin with milk. Serves 1 toddler.

Bear Mush Deluxe

Cook one serving of Bear Mush (Arrowhead Mills packaged cereal). Add 1 tablespoon of honey and ¼ cup of chopped fruit (peaches, apricots, pears, apples). Delicious on a cold winter morning.

French Toast

2 slices whole-wheat bread
1 egg
2 tablespoons milk

Beat egg and milk together in a pie pan. Dip bread in egg mixture and place in oiled skillet. Cook until lightly browned on each side. Good served with honey butter and cinnamon, or your favorite fruit preserves.

Honey Butter

½ cup honey
½ cup butter

Let butter soften at room temperature. Stir in honey with a fork. This is a great topping for waffles, pancakes, or French toast. Refrigerate after use.

Pita-Pinto Sandwich

½ cup mashed, cooked pinto beans (garbanzo or soy
  beans can also be used)
Tomato slices
Avocado slices
Shredded cheese
Pita bread

Spread the beans into the pita bread, add tomato, avocado, and cheese. Serve as is or put under broiler for 5 minutes.

Peanut Butter Deluxe Sandwich

Peanut butter
Applesauce
Raisins (pre-soaked for toddlers under age 2)
Crushed sunflower seeds

Mix all ingredients together and spread on whole-wheat bread.

Luncheon Bagels

Pizza bagel:

Spread bagel with *pizza sauce*
Top with *shredded mozzarella or provolone cheese*
Broil till cheese melts

Sprouts bagel:

Spread a lightly buttered, toasted bagel with:
   Sliced tomato
   Alfalfa sprouts
   Provolone cheese
Broil till cheese melts

Cream cheese bagel:

Spread a lightly buttered, toasted bagel with:
   Cream cheese
   Ground walnuts (optional)

Cheese Muffin

½ whole-wheat muffin, toasted and lightly buttered
1 slice cheese (Muenster, Swiss, provolone, or Colby)
1 slice tomato
1 tablespoon alfalfa sprouts

Layer toasted muffin half with tomato, sprouts, and then the cheese. Broil 2 minutes or until cheese melts. Be sure to serve after the cheese has cooled.

Cheese Tortillas

1 corn tortilla, buttered
Ricotta cheese or tofu
Grated Monterey Jack cheese
Sliced tomato

Place lightly buttered corn tortilla under the broiler for 2 minutes. Remove. Spread tortilla with ricotta or tofu, then tomato slices and top with the cheese. Broil until cheese melts. Cool to room temperature.

Cottage Cheese Delight

¼ cup cottage cheese
¼ cup puréed fruit (apples, pears, apricots, etc.)
2 tablespoons orange juice

Blend together and serve. This is a real favorite!

Applesauce 'n Raisins

8 pre-soaked raisins
½ cup applesauce

Blend in baby food grinder and serve.

Chickie Dip
Garbanzo (Chick-Pea) Dip

½ cup water
1 cup cooked garbanzos (chick peas), mashed
⅓ cup safflower oil
3 tablespoons sesame seeds
½ teaspoon sea salt
1 clove garlic, crushed
3 tablespoons lemon juice

Blend in blender or food processor. Use as a dip with veggies or crackers or as a sandwich spread.

Toddle Salad

1 apple
8 pre-soaked raisins
2 tablespoons shredded carrot
3 tablespoons yogurt
1 teaspoon honey

Cut apple into bite size pieces. Mix with raisins that have soaked overnight. Add carrot. Mix yogurt and honey and pour over salad. Serves 1.

Lentil Stew

1 tablespoon celery, chopped
½ potato, cubed
½ carrot, grated
1 tablespoon oil
¼ cup washed lentils
1¼ cup water or vegetable broth
1 tomato, chopped, or ½ cup tomato juice

Sauté celery, potato, and carrot in oil. Add lentils, water, and tomato. Bring to a boil. Cover and simmer 1 hour. Check to make sure liquid hasn't boiled out. Add more water, if needed.

Whole-wheat Biscuits

2 cups whole-wheat flour
2 tablespoons bran
1 tablespoon baking powder
¼ cup non-instant dry milk
½ teaspoon salt
⅓ cup safflower oil
¾ cup milk

Gently combine dry ingredients with wet ingredients. Knead 1 minute. Roll on floured cloth until ½-inch thick. Cut into biscuit shapes and place on baking sheet. Bake at 450°F for 10 minutes. Makes 1 dozen.

Corn Muffins

1 cup cornmeal
¼ cup whole-wheat flour
3 tablespoons soy flour (can be replaced with whole-
    wheat flour, but the soy flour adds extra protein)
2 teaspoons baking powder
1 teaspoon salt
1 egg
1 cup milk
3 tablespoons non-instant dry milk
3 tablespoons honey
3 tablespoons oil

Combine dry ingredients. Mix all liquid ingredients. Add liquid mixture to dry ingredients and beat well. Bake in muffin cups or well-greased muffin tin at 375°F for 20 minutes.

Peanut Butter Bread

2½ cups whole-wheat flour
1 tablespoon baking powder
1 teaspoon salt
1¼ cups milk
2 tablespoons oil
¼ cup honey
¾ cup peanut butter

Mix dry ingredients together. Set aside. Heat milk until warm. Add honey, oil, peanut butter to milk and stir well. Add liquid mixture to dry ingredients and blend well. Pour into well-greased bread pan and bake at 350°F for 40-50 minutes. Delicious served with mashed banana.

Raisin and Bran Muffins

3 cups bran
1 cup boiling water
2 eggs
1 cup honey
½ cup safflower oil
2 cups buttermilk
2¼ cups whole-wheat flour
2 teaspoons baking soda
½ teaspoon sea salt
½ cup raisins

Mix bran and boiling water in a large bowl and set aside. In another bowl, mix the eggs, honey, oil, and buttermilk. Add to the bran mixture. Sift together flour, baking soda and salt and stir into bran mixture. Add raisins. Bake at 375°F for 15 minutes. Serve with butter or honey.

Oatmeal Muffins

1½ cups buttermilk
2 cups oats
1 cup whole-wheat flour
1 teaspoon baking soda
½ teaspoon salt
2 eggs, beaten
3 tablespoons honey

Mix oats with buttermilk. Set aside. Sift dry ingredients together and add to oat mixture. Stir in eggs and honey. Let mixture stand 20 minutes before baking. Bake at 375°F for 15-20 minutes in oiled muffin tin. Makes 1 dozen.

Michael's Corn Tortillas

1½ cups water
3 tablespoons butter
1 cup cornmeal
1 cup whole-wheat flour
1 teaspoon salt

In a saucepan, bring water to a boil. Add butter. Stir in corn meal and cook over low heat for 5 minutes. Cool. Add salt to the flour and add to corn meal mixture. (Add more water or flour if necessary.) Divide dough into 10-12 pieces. Roll out on floured bowl into flat circles. Cook on a hot griddle or skillet 1½-2 minutes each side. Watch closely so they do not burn. Stack in a large plate and keep covered with a cloth. Delicious with your favorite beans or cheese.

Frozen Bananas

Banana
Orange juice

Insert a popsicle stick in the banana (or in ½ a large banana). Dip in orange juice. Wrap in plastic wrap and freeze.

Molly's Juice Bars

Pour juice (apple, orange, grape, apricot, papaya) into molds or cups with popsicle sticks. These are good for teething babies, but are sometimes difficult for them to hold alone. (You'll often find teething babies gnawing on the handles!)

Yogurt Popsicles

2 cups plain yogurt
1 6 ounce concentrated, unsweetened fruit juice (orange,
*   apricot, grape, apple)*
1 teaspoon vanilla

Mix well and freeze in popsicle molds or small paper cups with popsicle sticks. Great for teething babies.

Banana Splitz Pops

1 banana
1 cup plain yogurt
½ cup orange juice
Dash of vanilla or honey

Blend in blender and pour into popsicle molds. Freeze.

Banana Crunchsicles

1 banana
2 tablespoons melted carob chips
½ teaspoon safflower oil
1 teaspoon honey
Granola

Insert a popsicle stick into one end of the banana. Mix carob chips, oil, and honey together and melt over double boiler. (An egg poacher is perfect.) Roll in melted carob, then roll in granola. Freeze several hours.

Party Cubes

16 pineapple chunks
1 cup orange juice
1 cup cranberry juice
16 popsicle sticks

Place a small chunk of pineapple in each section of an ice cube tray. Mix juices together and pour over the pineapple. Insert a popsicle stick into each pineapple cube. Freeze.

Serve one party cube to each child on a warm day! Closely supervise so there are no children running with popsicle sticks in their mouth.

Special Day Sundae

1 scoop Haagan Dazs ice cream
1 banana, sliced
½ cup fresh strawberries, sliced
1 tablespoon carob chips
Whipped cream

Scoop ice cream into a dish. Cover with banana slices, strawberries, and carob chips. Top with fresh whipped cream.

Peanut Butter 'n Oatmeal Cookies

½ cup peanut butter
⅓ - ½ cup honey
1¼ cups old-fashioned oats
2 tablespoons dry milk
¼ teaspoon salt
¼ cup sunflower seeds (optional)

Mix peanut butter with honey. Add dry ingredients and mix. Drop by rounded teaspoon on greased baking sheet. Bake 10 minutes at 350°F. Makes 2½ - 3 dozen.

Oatmeal Cookies

1¾ cup flour
1 teaspoon sea salt
2 teaspoons baking powder
½ teaspoon cinnamon
⅓ cup safflower oil or softened butter
⅓ cup honey
⅓ cup molasses
2 eggs, beaten
2 cups old-fashioned oats
¾ cup raisins (optional) (not under age 2)

Sift together flour, salt, baking powder, and cinnamon. Combine oil, honey, molasses, and eggs in another large bowl. Add dry ingredients and mix well. Add oats and mix again. Gently stir in raisins. Drop by rounded teaspoonfuls on greased cookie sheet. Bake at 350°F for 10-12 minutes. Makes 4 dozen.

Laura's Playdough

(This is NOT to eat — but great for a rainy day project or a last minute birthday gift that children love.)

> 1 cup white flour
> ½ cup salt
> 2 tablespoons cream of tartar
> 1 tablespoon oil
> 1 cup water
> Few drops food coloring

Mix flour, salt, cream of tartar and oil in a saucepan. Add water and mix well. Cook over medium heat, stirring constantly, for 3 minutes. Dough will become difficult to stir and form a "clump" of dough. Knead for 5 minutes — add food color during kneading process. This keeps a long time if stored in a covered plastic container.

Kid's Stuff

(This recipe is NOT to eat — but another rainy day activity for toddlers to enjoy. Holiday ornaments can be crafted or any old shape can be cut from cookie cutters.)

> 3 cups flour
> 1½ cup cornstarch
> 1 cup water
> 1 tablespoon dry mustard or instant coffee

Combine dry ingredients in a large bowl. Pour in water, stirring constantly. Roll out on floured cloth or board and use cookie cutter for desired shapes — or shape and mold into shapes without cutting dough. Air dry molded objects or bake 1 hour at 350°F. For darker finish, brush first with milk and egg. Varnish when dry.

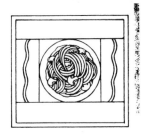

12 Whole Family Recipes

The "Family" section contains recipes for the entire family ages 3 to 103! Baby can follow a natural, nutritious, progression by eating foods from the previous chapters and then enjoy wholesome meals from "Family Foods". Many of these recipes can also be shared with a toddling two but check ingredients closely to be sure the recipe does not contain any "Foods That Could Cause Problems" (page 66).

Baked Apple Pancake

> 1 tablespoon margarine
> 3 cups peeled, cored, and sliced apples
> ½ teaspoon cinnamon
> ½ teaspoon allspice
> Juice from ½ lemon
> ½ cup whole-wheat flour
> ¾ teaspoon baking powder
> ¼ cup honey
> ¼ cup yogurt or crumbled tofu
> 2 eggs

Preheat oven to 400°F. Melt the margarine in a large saucepan or frying pan. Dump in the apples, cinnamon, allspice, and lemon juice. Mix gently. Cover pan. Turn heat to medium and bring to a boil. When boiling, turn heat to low and simmer, with the pan covered, for 10 minutes. Remove from heat. Combine the flour and baking powder in a small mixing bowl. Pour in the honey, yogurt or tofu, and eggs. Mix with a fork just until smooth, about ½ minute. Grease a 9-inch pie pan. Put about ⅓ of the batter in the bottom of the pie pan and spread around the bottom. Bake for 5 minutes. Remove from oven. Pour the apple mixture over the baked batter. Spoon the rest of the batter over the apples and spread evenly, making sure the batter touches the edges of the pan. Bake 20-25 minutes. Cut in wedges (like a pie). Eat while hot.

Family Whole-wheat Pancakes

¾ cup whole-wheat flour
2 teaspoons baking powder
½ teaspoon salt
1 tablespoon honey
1 cup milk (whole milk or buttermilk)
1 tablespoon oil
1 egg, beaten

Mix the dry ingredients together in one bowl and the wet ingredients in another. Add milk mixture to flour mixture, and stir just until moistened (any lumps will disappear during cooking). Pour by spoonfuls into oiled skillet. Flip over when bubbles come to the top. They are finished when a golden color appears. Top with fruit or preserves.

Berry Good Oatmeal

1 cup old-fashioned oats
2 cups water
¼ cup blueberries
½ cup apple juice

Bring water to boil. Sprinkle oats into water while stirring constantly. Cover and simmer 15-20 minutes. Remove from heat. Add berries and apple juice. Serves 2.

Special Day Cereal

¾ cup granola or Familia
1 scoop Haagan-Dazs ice cream
½ cup fruit (peaches, berries, bananas, strawberries)
¼ cup milk or yogurt

Put ice cream into cereal bowl. Cover with granola or Familia, fruit, and milk.

Avocado & Cheese Sandwich

Provolone cheese slices
Avocado slices
Tomato slices
Alfalfa sprouts or lettuce
Grated carrot
Safflower mayonnaise
Whole-wheat toast

Spread the toast with mayonnaise and add the cheese, avocado, tomato, sprouts, and grated carrot. Cut in half and serve.

To serve a toddler, make this an open-faced sandwich on one piece of toast and cut into fourths. Depending upon the age of the child, a lot of the sandwich will fall off. If this frustrates your child, you might try mashing up the avocado, bits of tomato, sprouts, and finely grated carrot and make a sandwich spread to put on the toast. Don't forget to add the cheese and mayonnaise.

Greek Pita Sandwich

Cut open a piece of whole-wheat pita bread so you have 2 flat pizza-like circles.

Top each half with:

Green pepper
Onion
Tomato
Mung bean sprouts
Sliced mushrooms

Top with grated mozzarella cheese — pop in broiler till cheese melts.

Egg Salad Sandwich

2 hard boiled eggs, chopped
1 tablespoon celery, chopped
1 tablespoon onion, chopped
Safflower mayonnaise
Vegetable salt
Alfalfa sprouts
Provolone cheese, shredded

Combine egg, celery, and onion in a small bowl with enough mayonnaise to bind together. Add vegetable salt to taste. Serve on pita bread, whole-wheat toast, or a bagel. This is good topped with sprouts and cheese.

Chick Pea Delight

2 cups cooked garbanzo beans
1 small clove garlic, crushed
2 tablespoons onion, chopped (green onions add color)
2 tablespoons green pepper, chopped
    or 2 tablespoons celery
    or both
½ package tofu, drained
2 tablespoons soy sauce or 1 tablespoon tamari sauce
3 tablespoons safflower mayonnaise

Mash garbanzo beans with a fork or quickly blend in blender or food processor. Add remaining ingredients and mix thoroughly.

This spread is delicious on whole-wheat toast with cheese, tomato, and sprouts or lettuce. It is also good served in whole-wheat pita bread.

Whole-wheat Bread

1 tablespoon dry yeast
2½ cups warm water
3 tablespoons honey
2 teaspoons sea salt
3 tablespoons safflower oil
6 cups whole-wheat flour

Dissolve yeast in water with 1 tablespoon of the honey. When bubbles rise to surface (2-3 minutes) add remaining 2 tablespoons honey and the oil. Mix salt and flour and add to mixture — about 1 cup at a time (use a wooden spoon for stirring). Knead for 10 minutes. Cover and let rise till double. Punch down, separate into 2 greased loaf pans. Cover and let rise again (1 hour). Bake 30 minutes at 350°F.

Sunflower Bread

2 tablespoons margarine
1 cup maple syrup or rice syrup
1 egg
¾ cup orange juice (preferably fresh)
2 tablespoons grated orange rind
1 tablespoon baking powder
½ teaspoon salt
2 cups whole-wheat flour
1 cup sunflower seeds, raw or toasted

Preheat oven to 325°F. Beat margarine, maple syrup or rice syrup, and egg with electric mixer for 1 minute in a medium-size bowl. Combine remaining ingredients together in a small bowl. Add to first mixture, all at once. Mix well with a wooden spoon just until smooth. Pour into greased 9"x5"x3" bread pan. Bake for 1 hour. Let cool in pan on rack 10-15 minutes. Turn out on rack to finish cooling. Wrap in foil to store.

Sesame Seed Salad Dressing

1/3 cup honey
1/2 teaspoon paprika
1/2 teaspoon salt
1/4 teaspoon dry mustard
1 teaspoon onion juice or finely grated onion
1/2 teaspoon Worcestershire sauce
1 cup oil
1/2 cup cider vinegar
1 tablespoon toasted sesame seeds

Blend all ingredients (except sesame seeds) in blender. Add seeds and mix with a spoon. This is a great "sweet and sour" dressing — especially good on spinach salads and falafel!

Taboulie

3/4 cup hot water
1 1/2 cups bulghur wheat
3 green onions, chopped
2 carrots, chopped
2 stalks celery, chopped
2 large tomatoes, chopped
1/4 cup lemon juice
1/3 cup safflower oil
1/2 teaspoon sea salt
2 tablespoons chopped mint (optional)
2 tablespoons chopped parsley (optional)
1/2 cup fresh alfalfa sprouts

Place bulghur in a large bowl. Add hot water, cover, and let stand while vegetables are being chopped. Prepare vegetables and add to the bulghur. Mix oil, lemon juice, and salt together and pour over the bulghur mixture. Chill at least one hour. Top with sprouts at serving time.

Spinach Salad

Spinach pieces, washed and dried
Mushrooms, sliced
Green onions, chopped
Mung bean sprouts
Hard boiled egg, sliced
Provolone cheese, grated

Toss all ingredients with Sesame Seed Salad Dressing and serve.

A toddler might like a plate with all these ingredients separated. Onions might not be a favorite with most, and the cheese could be cut in cubes instead of grated.

Antipasto Salad

3 cups leaf or Bibb lettuce, torn in small pieces
2 small tomatoes, quartered
1 cup fresh cauliflower, in bite-size pieces
½ cup grated carrot or 2 carrots cut into thin strips
½ cup pitted black olives
2 hard boiled eggs, quartered
½ cup cooked garbanzo beans
4 slices provolone cheese, cut into strips
1 small onion, sliced

Marinade

½ cup olive or safflower oil
¼ cup vinegar
½ teaspoon sea salt
Pinch oregano
1 garlic clove

Mix all marinade ingredients. Put cauliflower, olives, onions, and garbanzo beans in a dish and cover with the marinade. Refrigerate for 8 hours or overnight. Drain and save marinade. Arrange vegetables over lettuce pieces and add remaining ingredients. Toss lightly. Cover with remaining marinade or your favorite Italian dressing.

Potato Salad

6 or 7 medium potatoes
1 medium onion, chopped
2 hard boiled eggs, sliced
½ cup mayonnaise
1 teaspoon sea salt
¼ cup sunflower seeds

Cook potatoes in their skins, then pare and dice into bite-size pieces. Add onion, eggs, mayonnaise, and salt. Mix gently. Sprinkle sunflower seeds over the top and chill well before serving. This is a very refreshing summer salad!

Sprouts Salad

1 cup alfalfa sprouts
½ cup sunflower seeds, toasted
2 cups leaf and romaine lettuce
6 radishes or 1 cup radish sprouts
½ cucumber, sliced

Dressing

¼ cup oil
2 tablespoons vinegar
⅛ teaspoon salt

Toss salad ingredients together. Make dressing with oil, vinegar, and salt. Pour over salad and serve.

Summer Salad Dressing

1 tomato, quartered
1 cucumber, peeled and quartered
2 green onions (or 2 tablespoons chives)
½ cup oil
2 tablespoons vinegar
⅛ teaspoon sea salt
1 clove garlic, chopped

Blend all ingredients in the blender and chill 1 hour. Pour over tossed salad and enjoy!

Apple Salad

Apples
Celery, chopped
Walnuts
Raisins
Mayonnaise or yogurt

Wash and chop apples into bite-size pieces. Add celery, walnuts, and raisins. Add mayonnaise or yogurt and chill for 1 hour.

Fruit Salad

Grapes   Raisins
Bananas   Coconut
Oranges   Melon
Apples   Watermelon
Pineapple   Pears

Wash fruit and chop into bite-size pieces. Toss all fruit together in a large bowl and serve.

Spinach Dip

1 large bunch spinach, steamed lightly
½ cup chopped green onions
1 tablespoon parsley (optional)
½ teaspoon dill weed
1 cup yogurt or sour cream
1 cup mayonnaise
1 tablespoon lemon juice
¼ teaspoon chives
Dash thyme
¼ teaspoon salt

Blend all ingredients in blender. Chill in refrigerator overnight. Serve with your favorite fresh vegetables.

Veggie Platter

Broccoli flowerettes   *Cherry tomatoes*
Cauliflowerettes   *Zucchini pieces*
Carrot sticks   *Mushroom slices*
Celery sticks   *Radishes*
Green onions

Wash and prepare vegetables and arrange on a bed of lettuce.
Serve with your favorite dip.

Guacamole

1 *ripe avocado*
1 *tablespoon lemon juice*
1 *small tomato, diced*
1 *clove garlic, crushed*
½ *teaspoon chili powder*
Dash tabasco sauce

Mash avocado with a fork. Add remaining ingredients and
blend well. Chill one hour and serve with tortilla chips.

Potato Soup

¼ *cup oil*
1 *onion, chopped*
3 *carrots, grated*
1 *stalk celery, chopped*
7-8 *potatoes, diced (wash well and leave skins on)*
1 *quart stock or water*
1 *teaspoon vegetable salt*
1½ *cups dry milk powder (non-instant)*
½ *cup milk*

Sauté onions, carrots, celery, and bring potatoes in oil. Pour
in stock and vegetable salt. Bring to boil; simmer 1 hour or
cook 15 minutes in a pressure cooker. Add dry milk powder
to 2 cups of soup liquid and the ½ cup milk and blend quickly
in blender until milk powder is dissolved. Add to the soup and
simmer 5 minutes. Serve topped with grated Cheddar cheese.
Serves 4.

Cucumber Soup

4 cups cucumber, chopped
2 cups water
2 cups yogurt or sour cream
1 clove garlic, minced
1 tablespoon honey
1 teaspoon sea salt
¼ teaspoon dill
1 green onion, chopped

Put everything into blender or food processor and purée. Chill and serve. Serves 4.

Lentil Soup

2 tablespoons oil
2 cloves garlic, chopped
1 large onion, chopped
1 large carrot, grated
2 large potatoes, chopped small
1 cup washed lentils
3 cups tomato juice or 1 large can tomatoes
3 cups water or stock
Thyme
Vegetable salt
Optionals: corn; peas; grated Swiss cheese

Sauté garlic, onion, carrots, and potatoes in oil. Add remaining ingredients (adding thyme and vegetable salt to taste). Bring to a boil; then simmer 1 hour. Top with grated Swiss cheese.

This is our favorite soup recipe. If you've never tried lentils before, this is the perfect recipe to quickly learn to like this little bean! Serve with a good bread or corn tortillas — it makes a hearty meal!

Family Pizza

Crust:

1 tablespoon dry yeast
1¼ cups warm water
1 teaspoon honey
2 tablespoons oil
1½ teaspoons salt
3 - 3½ cups flour (whole-wheat or combination of unbleached and wheat)

Sauce:

2 cloves garlic
1 large onion, chopped
½ green pepper, chopped
1 can tomatoes (28-ounce)
1 can tomato purée (28-ounce)
Oregano
Salt
Pepper
Garlic powder
Basil
½ teaspoon baking soda

Cheese:

Mozzarella, shredded
Provolone, shredded

Dissolve yeast in water with honey. When yeast makes bubbles on surface, add oil and salt. Add flour a bit at a time —enough to make a stiff dough. Knead 10 minutes and let rise 1½ hours.

Sauté garlic, onion, and pepper in oil. Add remaining ingredients, except soda. Bring to boil, then sprinkle in soda and stir in. Simmer 1-2 hours.

Punch dough down and spread out on two (2) pizza pans. (Grease and flour pizza pans for best results.) Spread with sauce; add cheeses. Bake 15 minutes in pre-heated oven at 425°F.

Calzone

Dough:

1 tablespoon yeast
2 tablespoons honey
2 cups warm water
1 tablespoon salt
5½ - 6 cups flour

Filling:

1 lb. ricotta cheese
1 lb. slightly steamed spinach
2 cups grated mozzarella cheese
½ cup Parmesan cheese
2 cloves crushed garlic
½ cup minced onion
Salt
Pepper
Dash of nutmeg

Dissolve yeast in water with honey. Add salt and flour. Knead 10-15 minutes. Cover and set to rise 1 hour. Sauté garlic and onion in butter or oil. Add to cheese-spinach mixture. When dough has risen, punch down and divide into 8-10 balls. Roll each ball out into a circle ¼" thick. Fill with ½ to ¾ cup filling. (Place on ½ of circle, fold over, and make ½ inch rim). Moisten edges with water to help keep closed. "Crimp" with fork, and prick top several times. Bake on oiled tray in 450°F oven for 15-20 minutes. Brush with butter as soon as they come out of oven.

Spaghetti Sauce

2 cloves garlic, chopped
1 large onion, chopped
1 stalk celery, chopped
1 large carrot, grated
½ zucchini, grated
1 can tomatoes (28-ounce)
1 can tomato sauce (16-ounce)
1 can tomato paste (6-ounce)
½ cup water
Oregano
Basil
Salt
Pepper
Garlic salt

Sauté first five ingredients in oil. Add remaining ingredients. Simmer 2-3 hours. Add mushrooms during the last half hour if you wish. (Don't let the carrots and zucchini scare you away from this recipe; they add a lot of vitamins and fullness to the sauce.)

Ken's Spaghetti

6 medium eggs
½ pound Parmesan cheese, grated fine (about 2 cups)
3 medium onions, chopped
6 tablespoons olive oil
1 pound spaghetti or fettucine

Beat eggs until smooth. Stir in cheese. Mixture should have the consistency of a soft paste. Sauté onions in oil in a large skillet until soft. While the onions are cooking, cook spaghetti. Drain the spaghetti and pour back into the cooking pot. Mix the onion mixture with the spaghetti. Pour egg-cheese mixture paste over the spaghetti and stir all together quickly with two wooden spoons. The heat of the cooking pot and spaghetti will cook eggs slightly and melt the cheese. Avoid direct heat as this will cause the eggs to scramble. Serve immediately. Serves 4.

Spaghetti Squash

1 large spaghetti squash
1 quart spaghetti sauce (page 132)

Wash squash and pat dry with a towel. Pierce the skin of the squash several times with the point of a knife or a fork. Place on a cookie sheet and bake at 350°F for 1¼ - 1½ hours. (Test for tenderness by piercing with a fork.) Remove squash from the oven and cut lengthwise. Gently scoop out "spaghetti" strands and place in a large bowl. Cover with your favorite spaghetti sauce and sprinkle with Parmesan cheese. This is a delightful "natural" dinner everyone will enjoy! This is also a great substitute for those with a wheat or egg allergy.

Lasagna

1½ - 2 quarts spaghetti sauce
1 pound lasagna noodles
16 ounces ricotta cheese (or tofu or mixture of both)
2 eggs
Dash cinnamon
Dash nutmeg
½ teaspoon parsley (optional)
2 cups Mozzarella cheese, shredded
Parmesan cheese

Cook lasagna noodles while preparing cheeses. In a large bowl, combine ricotta cheese, eggs, cinnamon, nutmeg, and parsley and mix well. Set aside. Shred mozzarella cheese and place in another bowl. Have spaghetti sauce ready. Pre-heat oven to 350°F. In a large flat baking dish (oblong cake pans work well) place a layer of sauce, a layer of noodles, the ricotta cheese mixture (spread evenly over noodles), a layer of sauce, another layer of noodles, a layer of mozzarella cheese, a layer of sauce, another layer of noodles, more sauce, then sprinkle the top with Parmesan cheese. Bake at 350°F for 45 minutes. Cool 15 minutes before cutting.

Spinach Lasagna: Follow above recipe but add a layer of steamed spinach and ¼ cup sautéed chopped onions. Sprinkle ¼ cup Parmesan cheese over the spinach layer before adding the sauce.

Eggplant Parmesan

1 medium eggplant
⅓ cup flour
½ teaspoon sea salt
⅛ teaspoon cayenne pepper
1 tablespoon Parmesan cheese
2 tablespoons whole-wheat bread crumbs
¼ teaspoon dried parsley
1 egg
2 tablespoons milk
2 tablespoons oil
2 cups spaghetti sauce (see page 132)
1 cup mozzarella cheese, shredded
¼ cup Parmesan cheese, grated fine

Slice eggplant into ½ inch slices. Combine flour, salt, pepper, cheese, bread crumbs, and parsley. Mix egg and milk in a small bowl. Dip each eggplant slice into egg mixture, then the flour mixture, and then place in oiled skillet. Sauté eggplant until lightly browned on each side then drain slices on a paper towel. Arrange eggplant slices on a baking dish over one-half the spaghetti sauce. Pour remaining sauce over the top, then sprinkle with cheeses. Bake at 350°F for 20-30 minutes. Serves 4.

Spinach Sea Shells

¼ cup onion, chopped
1 clove garlic, crushed
1 pound fresh, washed spinach, chopped
1 pound ricotta cheese
10 ounces mozzarella cheese, shredded
⅓ cup Parmesan cheese
2 eggs, beaten
1 teaspoon sea salt
½ teaspoon oregano
1 quart spaghetti sauce
8 ounces large sea shells

Sauté garlic and onion in oil until soft. Add spinach and steam. In large bowl, combine cheeses, eggs, salt, and oregano. Gently stir in drained spinach mixture. Fill shells with spinach-cheese mixture and arrange in oiled baking dish. Cover with spaghetti sauce. Bake at 350°F for 40 minutes. Serves 4.

Enchilada Bake

6 corn tortillas
1½ - 2 cups cooked black (turtle) beans
3 tablespoons oil
1 small onion, chopped
1 clove garlic, crushed
½ green pepper, chopped
½ cup mushrooms, sliced (optional)
1 28 ounce can whole tomatoes
1 teaspoon ground cumin (optional)
2 teaspoons chili powder
½ teaspoon salt
1 cup Monterey Jack cheese, shredded
1 cup ricotta cheese
    or ½ cup ricotta and ½ cup tofu
Black olives, sliced (optional)

Sauté onion, garlic, green pepper, and mushrooms in the oil. Add tomatoes, cumin, chili powder, and salt, and simmer for 30 minutes. Line an oiled casserole dish with 3 corn tortillas, half of the beans, half of the sauce, half of the ricotta, and half of the Monterey Jack cheese. Repeat layers. Sprinkle sliced olives over the top. Bake at 350°F, uncovered, for 20 minutes.

Mexican Potato Bake

4 baked potatoes
2 cups refried black beans
1 cup shredded Cheddar cheese

Cut baked potatoes lengthwise. Place ½ cup of the beans into each potato, then top with ¼ cup cheese. Return to the oven for 5 minutes until the cheese melts.

Broccoli Quiche

Pastry for 9" pie
1 cup steamed broccoli
¼ cup sautéed mushrooms (optional)
1 cup Swiss cheese, grated
1 tablespoon finely chopped onion
4 eggs
1¾ cups cream or milk
½ teaspoon salt
⅛ teaspoon cayenne pepper
¼ teaspoon honey

Prepare pastry and line a 9" pie pan or quiche dish. Sprinkle cheese, onion, broccoli, and mushrooms into pie pan. Beat eggs with a fork, add remaining ingredients to eggs, and mix. Pour into pie pan. Bake 15 minutes at 425°F, then 30 minutes at 300°F. Quiche is done when a knife inserted 1" from the edge comes out clean. Let quiche stand 10 minutes before cutting. This is excellent served with a salad and muffins.

Crustless Quiche

½ cup sliced mushrooms
½ cup chopped onions
1 zucchini, chopped
1 clove garlic, chopped
2 tablespoons oil
5 eggs
⅓ cup milk
½ teaspoon sea salt
1 cup whole-wheat bread crumbs, cubed
4 ounces cream cheese, cut into small cubes
1 cup grated Cheddar cheese

Sauté mushrooms, onion, zucchini, and garlic in oil for 5 minutes. Combine eggs, milk, and salt in a small bowl and mix lightly. Gently stir in cheeses then add bread cubes. Pour into oiled 9-inch pie pan. Bake at 350°F for 45 minutes. Let cool 5 minutes before serving. Serves 4.

Falafel Burgers

2 cups cooked garbanzo beans
2 tablespoons oil
¼ cup onion, chopped
1 clove garlic, crushed
2 potatoes, cooked
2 tablespoons sesame butter
1 tablespoon lemon juice
1 tablespoon dry milk
2 teaspoons soy sauce
1 tablespoon parsley, chopped (optional)
½ teaspoon chili powder (optional)

Sauté onion and garlic in oil. Mash garbanzo beans and potato with fork or purée in blender or food processor. Add sautéed onion and garlic, sesame butter, lemon juice, dry milk, parsley, chili powder, and soy sauce.

Shape into patties and place on oiled cookie sheet. Bake in 350°F oven 10 minutes on each side. Serve in pita bread with lettuce, tomato, and cucumber.

Sesame seed dressing can be drizzled over sandwich for added flavor.

Note: Falafel is a Middle-Eastern food usually served on pita bread. This recipe can also be made into garbanzo balls and served as an appetizer or hors d'oeuvres.

Cabbage, Zucchini & Tomato Bake

½ cup chopped onion
1 tablespoon oil
1 head cabbage, chopped
2 zucchini, chopped
1 28-ounce can tomatoes

Sauté onion in oil until soft. Add cabbage and zucchini and steam for 10 minutes. (Add a bit of water to help steaming process if necessary.) Add tomatoes. Turn into casserole dish and bake 45 minutes in 350°F oven.

Easy Scalloped Potatoes

5 potatoes — sliced thin
2 tablespoons chopped onions
2½ cups milk
2 tablespoons flour
1 tablespoon butter
1 teaspoon sea salt

Place half of the potatoes in an oiled baking dish. Sprinkle with half of the onions, flour, salt, butter, and milk. Add remaining potatoes and the rest of the ingredients. Cover and bake at 350°F for 1 hour. Uncover and bake 30 minutes longer.

Zucchini Cheese Bake

2 medium unpared zucchini, sliced
2 large tomatoes, chopped
1 16 ounce can tomato sauce
½ teaspoon thyme
½ cup shredded provolone
1 clove garlic, minced

Combine all ingredients in an oiled baking dish. Bake at 350°F for 45 minutes. Serves 4.

Broiled Zucchini

1 zucchini
¼ cup Monterey Jack cheese, shredded
1 tablespoon Parmesan cheese

Wash and slice zucchini in ¼-inch pieces. Lightly steam in a steam basket or skillet for 5 minutes. Place zucchini slices on a foil-lined pie pan. Sprinkle with Monterey Jack, then Parmesan. Broil 5-7 minutes or until cheese melts. Serves 2.

Stuffed Baked Zucchini

2 medium zucchini
2 tablespoons oil
½ cup chopped onions
½ cup sunflower seeds, chopped
¾ cup yogurt
2 teaspoons lemon juice
¼ teaspoon sea salt
½ cup whole-wheat bread crumbs or ½ cup cooked
    brown rice
½ teaspoon parsley, chopped
1 tomato, chopped

Slice zucchini in half and scoop out the center, leaving a firm shell. Save the inside pulp. Sauté onion in oil until soft. Add the zucchini pulp and cook for 5 minutes. Add remaining ingredients and cook 5 more minutes. Spoon mixture back into zucchini shells and bake at 350°F for 20-30 minutes.

Cheesy Creamy Spinach

2 tablespoons butter
2 tablespoons flour
Dash cayenne pepper
⅛ teaspoon nutmeg
1½ cups milk
½ cup Parmesan cheese
1 pound fresh spinach, chopped
1 small onion, chopped
1 tablespoon oil

Make a white sauce with first six ingredients by melting butter in a saucepan then adding flour to make a paste. Slowly add milk and mix with a wire whip or a wooden spoon. Add cayenne, nutmeg, milk, and cheese and simmer 2 minutes. Pour over steamed spinach.

To steam spinach:
Wash spinach and drain well. Sauté onion in oil for 3 minutes, then add spinach and steam for 3 more minutes.

Zachary's Peanut Butter Balls

1 cup peanut butter
½ cup dry milk (not instant kind)
Some wheat germ (Mom says about ½ cup)
Some sesame seeds (about ⅓ cup)
¼ cup honey
Dash of vanilla

"Mix everything up all together real good. Roll them up into little balls. Put them in the refrigerator. Yummy! You can put raisins in them; my sister likes them like that, but I don't."

Variations:
1. Add ¼ cup carob chips and call the recipe "Peanut Butter Candy".
2. Instead of shaping into balls, press mixture into a square baking dish. Chill. Cut into "Peanut Butter Bars".

Caitlin's Berries 'n Cream

*1 cup berries (strawberries, blackberries, blueberries, rasp-
   berries)*
½ cup heavy cream
1 tablespoon honey
⅛ teaspoon vanilla extract

Wash berries and place them in a small bowl. Mix cream, honey, and extract together and pour over berries. Enjoy!

Red, White, & Blue Special

Haagan Dazs ice cream
Blueberries
Strawberries
Whipped cream

Cover ice cream with fruit and top with whipped cream. Great for the Fourth of July!

Tropical Banana Sundae

1 banana, sliced
1 tablespoon shredded fresh coconut
¼ cup milk or yogurt
1 tablespoon honey
Dash cinnamon

Mix all ingredients together in a small bowl. Serves 1.

Orange Fruit Punch

1 quart orange juice
½ apple, cored and pared
1 tablespoon lemon juice
¼ cup strawberries
1 tablespoon honey

Blend all ingredients in a blender and serve over ice. Serves 4.

Zachary's Own Shake

1½ cups milk
1 tablespoon carob powder
1 tablespoon honey
1 banana
¼ teaspoon lecithin
¼ teaspoon vanilla extract
2 tablespoons peanut butter

Mix all ingredients in blender on high speed until smooth and creamy. (This recipe was truly invented by an eight year old!)

Fruit Punches

Try these delicious juice combinations for a refreshing beverage:

orange/bananas/papaya

orange/lemonade/pineapple

orange/lemonade/grape

orange/apricot/pineapple

grapefruit/cranberry

grapefruit/pineapple

lemonade/lime-ade

lemonade/orange/grape

cranberry/apple/pineapple

melon/bananas/coconut

papaya/pineapple/orange

apricot/bananas

Invent your own combinations!

For special occasions or as a substitute for alcoholic beverages (good for pregnant women), try mixing your favorite juice(s) with a sparkling naturally carbonated water.

Tamari Nut Mix

2 cups sunflower seeds
1 cup pumpkin seeds
½ cup tamari sauce

Mix nuts with tamari sauce and let stand for 30 minutes. Bake on a baking sheet at 300°F for 15 minutes — stirring twice. Cool and store in airtight container. Delicious served with your favorite sandwich or just as a snack.

Fruit Leather

1 pound very ripe fruit (apples, apricots, peaches, pears, strawberries)
1 tablespoon honey

Wash, peel, and core fruit. Place fruit in blender or food processor and blend. Pour into saucepan, add honey, and heat mixture just until it boils, stirring frequently. Cook for 3 minutes. Line cookie sheets with a layer of plastic wrap. Pour fruit onto plastic and spread into a thin layer. Carefully stretch a layer of cheese cloth over tray, being careful to keep it off the fruit mixture. Place tray in the hot sun for about 8 hours (or place in electric oven on lowest heat). Fruit leather is done when it can be peeled away from plastic wrap. Roll into 6-inch strips, cool, and wrap with plastic wrap. This is a wonderful, natural, preservative-free treat everyone will love!

 # 13 Recipes for the Allergic Child

The following pages of recipes offer ideas for the parent who is coping with the nutritional needs of the allergic child. These recipes will be free of one or all of the following common food allergens: eggs, milk, and wheat. Be sure to check ingredients in recipes in all other sections of this book to find further foods for the allergic child.

Nut Milk Recipe

Use a blender to liquify 2 oz. ($1/3$ - ½ cup) of sesame seeds, raw cashews, or blanched almonds with 6 oz. (¾ cup) of water. Good for making "milk" shakes.

Soy Milk

Blend ¼ cup tofu with $2/3$ cup water in blender. Can be used for beverages or in baking.

Squash Milk

Dice and remove the seeds from a medium size yellow squash (but don't peel it). Measure 1¼ cups of the squash into blender jar. Pour in water just to cover the squash. Whirl in blender on high until smooth, about 1-2 minutes. Strain. Makes about 1 cup. Good for baking — especially in spice cake or pumpkin pie.

Nut Butters
(A peanut butter substitute for people who are allergic to peanuts)

1 cup ground nuts or seeds (almonds, sunflower seeds, or sesame seeds)
1 tablespoon safflower oil

Lightly toast ground nuts or seeds in a 300°F oven, stirring often. Place ¼ cup ground nut meal into the blender with a small amount of oil. Blend at high speed for 5 seconds. Gradually add remaining nut meal (¼ cup at a time) and oil and continue to blend. Stir mixture before each addition of nuts (be sure blender is turned off). Store nut butter in a glass jar in refrigerator. Use as peanut butter substitute or as a delightful addition to the diet.

Banana Shake

FREE OF:	● Egg	● Milk	● Wheat

1½ cups goat's milk* or nut milk
1 banana
Dash vanilla

Blend in blender at high speed until smooth.

* Check with your doctor. Some children can tolerate goat's milk even though they are lactose intolerant.

Tofu Mayonnaise

FREE OF:	● Egg		Milk		Wheat

8 ounces tofu
2 tablespoons cider vinegar
½ cup yogurt
1 tablespoon fresh lemon juice
1 teaspoon tamari*
1 tablespoon oil (safflower or olive)
½ teaspoon dry mustard
1 clove garlic, minced (optional)

Purée all ingredients in blender or food processor until smooth. Store in jar with tight fitting lid. Keeps in refrigerator for 1 week. Makes 1⅓ cups mayonnaise.

* For children on a wheat-free diet, omit tamari.

Tofu Dip

FREE OF:	● Egg	● Milk	● Wheat

8 ounces tofu
4 teaspoons fresh lemon juice
1 teaspoon onion juice or 1 clove minced garlic
¼ teaspoon dry mustard
¼ teaspoon sea salt
⅛ teaspoon celery seeds

Drain tofu well. Blend all ingredients in blender. Chill 1 hour. Good as a dip for vegetables and crackers and as a sour cream substitute on baked potatoes.

Peanut Butter-Tofu Deluxe

FREE OF:	●	Egg	●	Milk	●	Wheat

8 ounces tofu, drained
½ cup peanut butter
1 tablespoon honey
1 banana, mashed
¼ cup sunflower seeds, chopped (optional)
¼ cup raisins (optional)

Blend tofu, peanut butter, honey, and banana in blender or food processor. Add nuts and raisins if desired. Great on rice cakes, whole-wheat toast, or crackers.

Josh's Tofu Pancakes

FREE OF:	●	Egg	●	Milk		Wheat

¼ cup crumbled tofu
1½ cups water
1 tablespoon maple syrup
1 teaspoon vanilla
¼ cup oil
1½ cups whole-wheat flour
1½ teaspoons baking powder

Blend liquid ingredients in blender until smooth. Mix flour and baking powder together in medium-size bowl. Stir in liquid ingredients, mixing in gently just until the dry ingredients are dampened. Grease and heat a griddle or frying pan. Drop batter from a large spoon onto griddle, lightly spreading each cake with back of spoon to make a round cake. Cook until bottom of pancake is golden brown and edges of pancake begin to look dry. With spatula or pancake turner, loosen and turn cake, brown on other side. Serve at once with maple syrup or apple butter.

Buckwheat Pancakes

FREE OF:		Egg	●	Milk		Wheat

1½ cups buckwheat flour
2½ teaspoons baking powder
½ teaspoon sea salt
¼ cup safflower oil
¾ cup water
2 eggs, beaten
2 tablespoons honey

Combine all dry ingredients in a large bowl. Mix oil, water, eggs, and honey. Stir liquid ingredients into the dry ingredients. Pour batter onto oiled griddle or skillet. Flip when brown on one side. Enjoy! Serves 3-4.

Rice Pancakes

FREE OF:	●	Egg	●	Milk	●	Wheat

2 cups cooked brown rice
2 cups tofu, drained and chopped
2 tablespoons lemon juice
1 teaspoon sea salt
2 tablespoons potato flour
¼ cup chopped walnuts (optional)

Mix rice and tofu together in a large bowl. Add remaining ingredients. Shape into 4-6 "pancakes" and cook in oiled skillet. Fry until golden on each side. Delicious for breakfast, lunch, or supper.

Rice Waffles

FREE OF:		Egg	●	Milk	●	Wheat

2 cups rice flour
2 cups goat's milk* or diluted non-dairy creamer (free of
    casein, sodium caseinate, or lactolbumin)
4 teaspoons corn-free baking powder
½ teaspoon sea salt
¼ cup oil or milk-free margarine
2 eggs, separated

Mix all ingredients except eggs in a large bowl. Gently mix egg yolks with a fork and oil to batter. Beat egg whites until stiff and gently fold into batter. Cook on lightly oiled skillet or griddle. Serves 4.

* Check with your doctor. Some children can tolerate goat's milk even though they are lactose intolerant.

Rye Bread

FREE OF:	●	Egg	●	Milk	●	Wheat

1 tablespoon dry yeast
1¼ cups warm water
1 teaspoon honey
4 cups rye flour
2 teaspoons salt
2 tablespoons safflower oil
3 tablespoons caraway seeds (optional)

Dissolve yeast with water and honey. Add oil. Stir in dry ingredients adding more water if necessary. Knead 10 minutes. Cover and let rise in a warm place for 1½ hours. Punch down. Knead 5 minutes, shape into 1 loaf, and place in greased bread pan. Cover and let rise 30 minutes. Bake 1 hour and 10 minutes in 375°F.

Wonderful Wheatberry Bread

FREE OF:	●	Egg	●	Milk		Wheat

¾ cup whole wheat berries
2 cups water
1 cup whole-wheat flour
1 cup chopped nuts
1 teaspoon baking soda
1 teaspoon salt
½ cup crumbled tofu
½ cup water
¼ cup barley malt or maple syrup
2 tablespoons oil

Combine whole-wheat berries and water in medium size saucepan. Bring to boil over medium heat and boil for 2 minutes. Turn off heat, cover saucepan, and let stand for 1-2 hours. Bring to boil again and simmer, uncovered, 1½ hours or until tender.

Preheat oven to 350°F. Mix flour, nuts, baking soda, and salt in a large bowl. Place tofu, water, barley malt or maple syrup, and oil in blender and blend until smooth. Stir tofu mixture into flour mixture and mix just until dry ingredients are all moistened. Drain whole-wheat berries and fold into bread mixture. Pour into greased 8"x4" bread pan. Bake 1 hour. Let cool in pan for 10 minutes, then turn out on wire rack to finish cooling.

Banana Nut Bread

FREE OF:		Egg	●	Milk	●	Wheat

1½ cups banana, mashed
2 tablespoons water
2 eggs
1½ cups arrowroot flour
1 teaspoon soda
½ teaspoon sea salt
¾ cup walnuts, chopped

Combine banana and water in a large bowl. Beat eggs; then mix with banana. Stir in dry ingredients and mix well. Add chopped nuts. Bake at 350°F for 45 minutes in a lightly greased bread pan.

Oatmeal Bran Muffins

FREE OF:		Egg	●	Milk		Wheat

1 cup oatmeal
1 cup bran or whole wheat flour
1 tablespoon baking powder
1 teaspoon baking soda
½ teaspoon salt
1 egg
3 tablespoons oil
2 tablespoons barley malt or molasses
1 cup soft tofu or soy yogurt
½ cup chopped nuts (preferably toasted)
½ cup currants or raisins

Preheat oven to 425°F. Put the oatmeal, bran or flour, baking powder, baking soda and salt in a blender. Blend on high speed about 1 minute or until it looks like flour. Dump into a large mixing bowl. Put remaining ingredients, except currants and nuts in blender and blend about 1 minute or until smooth. Pour blended mixture over oatmeal mixture; mix gently until all the dry ingredients are moistened. Stir in nuts and currants or raisins. Pour into greased or paper-lined muffin cups. (Cups will be about ¾ full.) Bake 15 minutes. Turn out onto wire rack to cool.

Peanut Butter Carob Fudge

FREE OF:	●	Egg		Milk	●	Wheat

1 cup peanut butter
1 cup honey
¾ cup toasted carob powder
¾ cup non-instant dry milk powder

Mix all ingredients together with a fork then knead about 3 minutes to thoroughly combine mixture. Press batter into square pan (9″x9″) and refrigerate several hours or overnight. Cut into squares and serve. Raisins can be added for a variation.

Banana-Oat Cake

FREE OF:		Egg	●	Milk	●	Wheat

2 cups oat flour (or ground old-fashioned oats)
2 teaspoons corn-free baking powder
½ teaspoon sea salt
2 tablespoons safflower oil
2 eggs
⅓ cup honey
2 tablespoons water
2-3 bananas, mashed

Sift oat flour before measuring, then sift with baking powder and salt. Beat egg, oil, and honey in a small bowl. Add mashed banana to egg mixture and mix well. Combine liquid and dry ingredients together. Pour into greased square pan (8″x8″) and bake at 350°F for 30 minutes.

Oatmeal Sheet Cake

FREE OF:	● Egg	● Milk	● Wheat

1 cup oat flour (or old-fashioned oats, ground fine)
1 tablespoon arrowroot
1 teaspoon cinnamon
1 teaspoon salt
½ teaspoon nutmeg
⅔ cup water
2 teaspoons corn-free baking powder
2 tablespoons safflower oil
1 banana, mashed
⅓ cup almonds or walnuts
¼ cup raisins

Mix all ingredients in a large bowl. Pour into greased square baking pan (9"x9"). Bake at 450°F for 15-20 minutes.

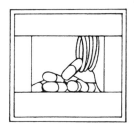# 14 What *Not* to Put into the Mouths of Babes

Over five million children are poisoned each year in the United States. Infants, toddlers, and children need not be out of sight very long before they can inhale or ingest a toxic substance.

Consider these facts, according to Scott Wiley, Manager of the Blue Ridge Poison Control Center at the University of Virginia:

- Poisonings are most likely to occur in children under five years of age, with ages three and under having the highest number of poisonings reported.
- There is an extremely high incidence of repeated poisonings. A child who is poisoned once probably will be poisoned again.
- A very large number of ingested poisons are medications found within a child's reach or climb. (Give a toddler a chair, desk, toilet, or table to stand or climb on and he probably will.)
- Many first aid antidote charts and labels are incorrect or out-of-date. Often a well-meaning parent does more harm than good by following directions from a chart rather than phoning the Poison Control Center or a physician first. In fact, the old remedy of giving salt water to induce vomiting has even caused death.
- Never give syrup of ipecac to induce vomiting unless directed to do so by the Poison Control Center or a physician. Every medicine cabinet should contain a bottle of ipecac syrup. Check expiration date to be sure your bottle is not outdated.

[155]

First Aid for Poisoning

SWALLOWED POISONS
If the person is awake and able to swallow, give water.
Call the poison center or your doctor.
Caution: Antidote charts and labels may be incorrect. *Do not*
give salt, vinegar, mustard, raw eggs, or citrus juices.

INHALED POISONS
Immediately drag or carry the person to fresh air.
Ventilate the area.
Call the poison center or your doctor.

POISONS ON THE SKIN
Remove contaminated clothing and flood skin with water for
15 minutes.
Wash gently with soap and water twice.
Call the poison center or your doctor.

POISONS IN THE EYE
Flush the eye with lukewarm (not hot) low pressure water for
15-20 minutes. Water can be poured from a pitcher held 2-3
inches from the eye. You need not force the eyelid open but
have the patient blink while flushing.
Call the poison center or your doctor.

Poison-Proofing Your Home

1. Do you have the phone number of your Poison Control
   Center or physician by your phone(s)? If not, please put
   this book down and do it now!! Your child is precious . . .
2. Store all medicines and household cleaning supplies out
   of reach (and sight!) of children. Use locked cabinets or
   child-resistant safety latches when necessary.
3. Request child-resistant caps on all medicines. Request
   extra containers and transfer vitamins into them.
4. Never store medicine or any poisonous product in beverage or food bottles. More than one unsuspecting child has
   picked up a soda bottle in the garage that was filled with
   gasoline or kerosene.
5. Never tell children that medicine tastes like candy. That
   causes confusion and possible poisoning. It also is wise to
   take your own medicine when children aren't watching
   since they love to imitate grown-ups.

6. Check the dates of all drugs in your medicine cabinet and flush old pills down the toilet. Do not let your child play with empty medicine bottles.
7. Keep a bottle of ipecac syrup in your medicine cabinet. **Caution:** Use ipecac *only* if instructed to do so by the poison control center or a physician. Follow their specific instructions for use.
8. Be aware of which plants are poisonous. The following plants are poisonous:

azalea	laurels
acorns	lily-of-the-valley
autumn crocus	mistletoe
baneberry	monkshood
bittersweet	morning glory
bleeding heart	mushrooms
boxwood	narcissus
buckeye	nightshade
buttercup	oak
caladium	oleander
*castor bean	periwinkle
choke cherry	philodendron
crocus	poison ivy
daffodil	poison oak
dieffenbachia	poison sumac
elderberry	pokeweed
elephant ear	poppy
English ivy	privet
four-o-clocks	rhododendron
*foxglove	rhubarb leaves
golden chain	rosary pea
holly	shamrock
hyacinth	sweet pea
iris	tobacco
jequirity bean	tomato leaves
jessamine	tulip
Jerusalem cherry	*water hemlock
Jimson weed	*wild mushroom
juniper	wisteria
larkspur	yew

*especially toxic plants

Check with your Poison Control Center if you have a question about plants not listed above.

BEWARE . . . the following products can cause POISONING:

aftershave lotion
alcohol
ammonia
antifreeze
aspirin
automatic dishwashing
  compound
automotive products
bleach
charcoal lighter
chemicals
cigarettes
cleaning and disinfecting
  agents
cosmetics
cough medicine
drain cleaner
drugs (prescription or
  over-the-counter drugs,
  ointments, and creams)
furniture polish
gasoline

glues and adhesives
hair dyes and bleaches
insecticides
jewelry containing beans or
  seeds
kerosene
lye
moth balls
mouthwash
nail polishes and removers
oven cleaners
paint and paint thinners
perfumes
pesticides
petroleum products
plants
plastics
rat poison
rubbing alcohol
shampoo and soap
toilet bowl cleaner
vitamins and minerals
weed killer

Other products also can be harmful. When in doubt, consult the Poison Control Center in your area.

Curiosity killed the cat. Don't let it kill your child. Put all poisons out of the reach of children!

Bibliography

Ballentine, Rudolph, M.D. *Diet and Nutrition.* Himalayan International Institute: Honesdale, Pa., 1978

Castle, Sue. *The Complete New Guide to Preparing Baby Foods.* New York: Doubleday & Company, Inc., 1981.

Davis, Adelle. *Let's Cook It Right.* New York: Signet, 1947.

Davis, Adelle. *Let's Get Well.* New York: Harcourt, Brace, and World, Inc., 1965.

Davis, Adelle. *Let's Have Healthy Children.* New York: Harcourt, Brace, and World, Inc., 1951.

Dufty, William. *Sugar Blues.* New York: Chilton, 1975.

Emerling, Carol G. and Eugene O. Jonckers. *The Allergy Cookbook.* Garden City, NY: Doubleday & Company, Inc., 1969.

Ewald, Ellen. *Recipes for a Small Planet.* New York: Ballantine, 1973.

Feingold, B. F. *Why Your Child Is Hyperactive.* New York: Random House, 1974.

Ford, Marjorie Winn, Susan Hillyard, and Mary Faulk Kooch. *The Deaf Smith Country Cookbook.* New York: Collier Books, 1973.

Goldbeck, Nikki and David. *The Supermarket Handbook: Access to Whole Foods.* New York: Harper and Row, 1973.

Golos, Natalie and Frances Golos Golbitz. *Coping with Your Allergies.* New York: Simon and Schuster, 1979.

Heslin, Jo-Ann, Annette B. Natow, and Barbara C. Raven. *No-Nonsense Nutrition for Your Baby's First Year*. Boston, C.B.I. Publishing Company, Inc., 1978.

Hirschfeld, Herman, M.D. *Understanding Your Allergy*. New York: Arco Publishing, Inc., 1979.

Hostage, Jacqueline. *Living . . . Without Milk*. White Hall, VA: Betterway Publications, 1981.

Kende, Margaret and Williams, Phyllis. *The Natural Baby Food Cook Book*. Los Angeles, CA: Nash Publishing Corporation, 1972.

Kropf, William, M.D. and Milton Houben. *Harmful Food Additives The Eat Safe Guide*. Port Washington, NY: Ashley Books, Inc., 1980.

LaLeche League. *The Womanly Art of Breastfeeding*. Interstate Printers, 1958.

Lappé, Frances Moore. *Diet for a Small Planet*. New York: Ballantine, 1975.

Nonken, Pamela P. and S. Roger Hirsch, M.D. *The Allergy Cookbook and Food-Buying Guide*. New York: Warner Books, 1982.

Pryor, Karen. *Nursing Your Baby*. New York: Pocket Books, 1974.

Rapaport, Howard G., M.D. and Shirley Motter Linde. *The Complete Allergy Guide*. New York: Simon and Schuster, 1970.

Robertson, Laurel, Carol Flinders, and Bronwen Godfrey. *Laurel's Kitchen: A Handbook for Vegetarian Cookery and Nutrition*. Berkeley, CA: Nilgiri Press, 1976.

Rapp, Doris J., M.D. *Allergies and the Hyperactive Child*. New York: Sovereign Books, 1979.

Rapp, Doris J., M.D. *Allergies and Your Child*. New York: Holt, Rinehart and Winston, 1972.

Smith, Lendon, M.D. *Feed Your Kids Right*. New York: McGraw-Hill Book Company, 1979.

Smith, Lendon, M.D. *Foods for Healthy Kids*. New York: Berkeley Books, 1981.

Somekh, Emile, M.D. *Allergy and Your Child*. New York: Harper and Row, 1974.

Thomas, Anna. *The Vegetarian Epicure*. New York: Vintage Books, 1972.

Toth, Robin. *Naturally It's Good . . . I Cooked It Myself!* White Hall, VA: Betterway Publications, 1982.

Toth, Robin and Jacqueline Hostage. *Does Your Lunch Pack Punch?* White Hall, VA: Betterway Publications, Inc., 1983.

Wunderlich, Ray C. *Improving Your Diet*. St. Petersburg, FL: Johnny Reads, Inc., 1976.

Yntema, Sharon. *Vegetarian Baby*. Ithaca, NY: McBooks Press, 1980.

Yoga Fellowship Society. *Make It Light*. Boardman, OH: Nature's Nook, 1980.

Index

Additives, as cause of allergy, 68
  twenty worst, 69
Allergies and Your Child, 68
Allergy, defined, 68
Allergy, food, 67-74
  most common causes, 66, 68
  treatment of, 70
  foods least likely to cause, 68
  symptoms of, 60, 69
Allergy Basic Four Food Groups
  (chart), for those with food
  allergies, 54
Amino acids, 40
Antigen, defined, 67
Arrowroot, 28

B-vitamins, importance of during
  pregnancy, 37
Baby food grinder, 22
Baby food, commercial, 11
  home prepared, advantages of, 19
  preparation, items needed, 21
  storage, items needed, 21
Baby's Food Diary (chart), fill-in,
  75-76
Bags, plastic freezer, 23
Baking powder, 28
Basic Four Food Groups (chart),
  for diets that include meat, 52
Basic four food groups, 39-40
Bean Preparation (chart), 92-93
Beans, introducing, 61
Beginners, feeding tips, 77
Bibliography, 159-161
Bibs, 23
Blender, 22
Bottle feeding, advantages and
  disadvantages, 58
  helpful hints, 57
Breads and crackers, some good
  brands, 32
Breast feeding, 55-58
  advantages and disadvantages, 58
  importance of diet, 55
  responsibilities of, 55
Breast feeding-formula combination,
  57

Calcium, function of, 47
  good sources of, 47
  need for during pregnancy, 36
Carbohydrates, 42
Carob, 27
Cereal, introducing, 60
  natural, 28
  some good brands, 33
Charts
  Allergy Basic Four Food Groups, 54
  Baby's Food Diary, fill-in, 75-76
  Basic Four Food Groups, 52
  Bean Preparation, 92-93
  Better Nutrition Substitutions, 26
  Cooking Grains, 94
  Food Combinations that Form
    Complete Proteins, 51
  Foods that Could Cause Problems,
    66
  Good Foods for Baby or Toddler,
    32-33
  Meatless Basic Four Food Groups,
    53
  Notes on Favorite Natural Foods,
    fill-in, 34
  Sprout Growing, 98-99
  That First Year . . . A Time Table for
    Introducing Solid Foods, 64-65
Cheese, introducing, 61, 83, 89
  natural, 27
Colors, natural, 27
Complementary proteins, 40
Cooking Grains (chart), 94
Cornmeal, yellow, 30
Crackers and breads, some good
  brands, 32
Cup, spouted, 24

Dairy products, some good brands, 33
Diet for a Small Planet, 16, 40
Dish, heated, 24

Eating habits, establishing good, 50
Egg Free Diet, foods to avoid, 72-73
Eggs, introducing, 61, 83

Fat-soluble vitamins, 44
Father, role of in feeding, 15
Fats and oils, natural sources of, 43
Feed Your Kids Right, 70
Feeding, basic philosophy, 62-63
    starting solids, 59-61
    time table for introducing new
        foods, 64
Finger foods, introducing, 105
First Aid for poisoning, 156
Flavoring, natural, 27
Folic acid deficiency, 37
**Food Combinations that Form
    Complete Proteins** (chart), 51
Food mill, 22
Food processor, 22
Food, as cause of allergies, 68
    list of natural, 25
    substitutions for better nutrition, 26
Foods for Healthy Kids, 70
Foods that Could Cause Problems
    (chart), 66
Formula, of iron fortified, 57
Formula-breast feeding combination,
    57
Fruit beverages, introducing, 83
Fruits and juices, some good brands, 32
Fruits, introducing, 60, 78, 105

Grains, introducing, 78, 89, 105
Grater, 22

Harmful Food Additives, 69
Health food store, shopping in, 31
Heredity, role in allergies, 68
Heslin, Jo-Ann, 49
High chair, 24
Honey, 29
Hostage, Jacqueline, 71
Houben, Milton, 69

Intolerance, food (see also:
    "Allergies"), 67

Jams and spreads, some good brands,
    32
Jars, glass, 23
Juices and fruits, some good brands, 32

Kropf, Dr. William, 69

Lact-Aid™, 71
Lacto-Ovo vegetarian, defined, 40
Lacto-Vegetarian, defined, 41
Lactose (milk sugar), 60
Lactose intolerance, 71
LaLeche League, The, 55
Lappé, Francis Moore, 16, 40

Legumes, introducing, 89
Linoleic acids, good sources of, 43
Living Without Milk, 71
Lunch box, 24

Magnesium, function, 49
    good sources of, 49
Mayonnaise, safflower, 28
Meatless Basic Four Food Groups
    (chart), for Lacto-Ovo vegetarian
    diets, 53
Menu, for advanced (10-12 months),
    90
    for beginners (4-6 months), 78
    for intermediates (7-9 months), 84
    planning, 17
Milk allergy, 71-72
Milk-Free Diet, foods to avoid, 71
Minerals, function of, 47
    good sources of, 47
Modified starch, in commercial baby
    food, 19
Molasses, 29

Natural foods, fill-in list of favorite, 34
Nausea, during pregnancy, 37
*No-Nonsense Nutrition for Your Baby's
    First Year*, 49
Nursing Your Baby, 49, 55
Nutrients, 41
Nutrition, importance of, 39

Obesity, dangers of, 50
Oils and fats, 43
    natural sources of, 43
    unrefined, 29

Peanut butter, 28
Phosphorus, function of, 48
    good sources of, 48
Poison Control Center, 155
Poisoning, first aid for, 156
Poison-proofing your home, tips,
    156-157
Poisonous plants, list of, 157-158
Poisonous products, list of 158
Potassium, function of, 48
    good sources of, 48
Pregnancy, importance of nutrition,
    35-37
    need for calcium, 36
    need for protein, 36
    weight gain during, 35
Pressure cooker, 22
Protein, 38, 42
    need for, 36, 40
Proteins, combining incomplete, 40
Pryor, Karen, 49, 55

Rapp, Doris, 68
Recipes, see *Recipe Index* below
Rice, brown, 31

Sea salt, 29
Smith, Dr. Lendon, 70
Sodium, function of, 48
  good sources of, 48
Spoon, baby, 23
Spreads and jams, some good brands, 32
Sprout Growing (chart), 98-99
Starch, natural sources, 42
Steam baskets, 22
Stress, ill-effects on unborn, 37
Substitution for better nutrition, 26
Sugar, natural sources, 42
Supermarket Shopper's Guide (chart), 32

That First Year . . . A Timetable for Introducing Solid Foods (chart), 64-65
Thermos, 24
Tofu, introducing, 83
  storing, 87
Toxemia, 36

Vanilla, 29
Vegan, defined, 40
Vegetables, fresh, 27
  introducing, 60-61, 83, 89, 105

Vegetarian diet, 40
  advantages of, 16
  cautions, 41
Vitamin A, function of, 45
  good sources of, 45
  symptoms of overdose, 44
Vitamin B Complex, function of, 45
  good sources of, 45
Vitamin C, function of, 46
  good sources of, 46
Vitamin D, function of, 46
  good sources of, 46
  symptoms of overdose, 45
Vitamin E, function of, 46
  good sources of, 46
Vitamin K, function of, 47
  good sources of, 47
Vitamins, 44-49
  natural, advantages of, 44
  synthetic, 44
  types of, 44

Water, importance of, 49
  sources for baby, 49
Water-soluble vitamins, 44
Wheat flour, substitutions for, 74
Wheat-Free Diet, foods to avoid, 73-74
Whole-wheat flour, 30
Wiley, Scott, 155
Wunderlich, Dr. Ray C., 11-13

Yogurt, introducing, 60, 83

Recipe Index

Antipasto Salad, 125
Apple Delight, 97
Apple Salad, 127
Appled Sweet Pótatoes, 101
Applesauce 'n Raisins, 111
Avocado & Cheese Sandwich, 121
Avocado Banana Cream, 79
Avocado-ado!, 78

Baby Rice Pudding, 88
Baby Vegetable Purée, 84
Baby's 1st Birthday Cake, 103
Baked Acorn Squash, 101
Baked Apple Pancake, 119
Baked Sweet Potatoes, 100
Banana Crunchsicles, 116
Banana Nut Bread, 152
Banana Shake, 146
Banana Splitz Pops, 116

Banana-ana!, 79
Banana-Oat Cake, 153
Barley Cereal, 81
Beaçs, cooking timetable, 92-93
  how to cook, 93
Bear Mush Deluxe, 109
Berry Good Oatmeal, 120
Beverages
  Banana Shake, 146
  Brown Monkey Shake, 107
  Carob Delight, 107
  Carob Milk, 106
  Cranberry Punch, 107
  Fruit Punches, 143
  Orange Fruit Punch, 142
  Simple Banana Smoothie, 86
  Smoothies, 86
  Sunny Smoothie, 106
  Zachary's Own Shake, 142

Bread(s)
Banana Nut Bread, 152
French Toast, 109
Michael's Corn Tortillas, 115
Peanut Butter Bread, 113
Rye Bread, 150
Sunflower Bread, 123
Whole-wheat Biscuits, 112
Whole-wheat Bread, 123
Wonderful Wheatberry Bread, 151
Broccoli & Rice, 91
Broccoli Quiche, 136
Broiled Zucchini, 138
Brown Monkey Shake, 107
Buckwheat Pancakes, 149
Bulgur & Vegetables, 90
Bunny Yogurt, 100
Bunny Yogurt II, 100

Cabbage, Zucchini & Tomato Bake, 137
Caitlin's Berries 'n Cream, 141
Cake(s)
Baby's 1st Birthday Cake, 103
Cream Cheese Icing, 103
Gingerbred Shortcake, 104
Banana-Oat Cake, 153
Oatmeal Sheet Cake, 154
Calzone, 131
Carob Delight, 107
Carob Milk, 106
Carrot 'n Bean Soup, 91
Carrot Salad, 99
Carrot-Zucchini Shred, 100
Cereal(s)
Barley Cereal, 81
Bear Mush Deluxe, 109
Berry Good Oatmeal, 120
Combination Cereal, 82
Corn Meal Cereal, 108
Granola, 108
Millet Cereal, 81
Oatmeal, 81
Oatmeal Plus, 87
Rice Cereal, 81
Rice, Oat, or Barley Cereal, 82
Special Day Cereal, 120
Cheese Muffins, 110
Cheese Tortillas, 111
Cheesy Creamy Spinach, 139
Chick Pea Delight, 122
Chickie Dip, 111
Colorful Barley, 95
Combination Cereal, 82
Cookies
Oatmeal Cookies, 117
Peanut Butter 'n Oatmeal Cookies, 117
Corn Meal Cereal, 108
Corn Muffins, 113

Cottage Cheese Delight, 111
Cottage Cheese Lunch, 88
Cottage Cheese Pancakes, 97
Cranberry Punch, 107
Cream Cheese Icing, 103
Crustless Quiche, 136
Cucumber Soup, 129

Desserts
Banana Crunchsicles, 116
Banana Splitz Pops, 116
Frozen Bananas, 115
Molly's Juice Bars, 115
Party Cubes, 116
Peanut Butter Carob Fudge, 153
Red, White, & Blue Special, 141
Special Day Sundae, 117
Tropical Banana Sundae, 142
Yogurt Popsicles, 115
Zachary's Peanut Butter Balls, 141
Dried Fruit Purée, 80

Easy Scalloped Potatoes, 138
Egg Salad Sandwich, 122
Eggplant Parmesan, 134
Egg(s)
Broccoli Quiche, 136
Crustless Quiche, 136
Meredith's Omelet, 97
Elizabeth's Peanut Butter Pudding, 101
Enchilada Bake, 135

Falafel Burgers, 137
Family Pizza, 130
Family Whole-wheat Pancakes, 120
French Toast, 109
Frozen Bananas, 115
Fruit, cooking times for dried, 80
    cooking times for fresh, 79
Fruit Leather, 144
Fruit Punches, combinations, 143
Fruit Purée, 79
Fruit Salad, 127
Fruit Yogurt, 86
Fruit(s)
Apple Delight, 97
Applesauce 'n Raisins, 111
Avocado Banana Cream, 79
Avocado-ado!, 78
Banana-ana!, 79
Caitlin's Berries 'n Cream, 141
Dried Fruit Purée, 80
Fruit Purée, 79
Fruit Yogurt, 86
Tofu-Banana Whip, 87

Garden Casserole, 95
Gingerbread Shortcake, 104
Grains, how to cook, 94

Grain(s)
Bulgur & Vegetables, 90
Colorful Barley, 95
Lentils & Rice, 90
Rice 'n Beans, 91
Rice-Squash, 94
Granola, 108
Greek Pita Sandwich, 121
Guacamole, 128

Homemade Yogurt, 85
Honey Butter, 109

Josh's Tofu Pancakes, 148

Ken's Spaghetti, 132
Kid's Stuff, 118

Lasagna, 133
Laura's Playdough, 118
Lentil Cheeseburgers, 95
Lentil Soup, 129
Lentil Stew, 112
Lentils & Rice, 90
Luncheon Bagels, 110

Main Dishes
Calzone, 131
Enchilada Bake, 135
Family Pizza, 130
Ken's Spaghetti, 132
Lasagna, 133
Mexican Potato Bake, 135
Spaghetti Sauce, 132
Spinach Lasagna, 133
Spinach Sea Shells, 134
Stuffed Baked Zucchini, 139
Meredith's Omelet, 97
Mexican Potato Bake, 135
Michael's Corn Tortillas, 115
Milk substitutes, Nut Milk, 145
Soy Milk, 145
Squash Milk, 145
Millet Cereal, 81
Molly's Juice Bars, 115
Muffins
Corn Muffins, 113
Oatmeal Bran Muffins, 152
Oatmeal Muffins, 114
Raisin and Bran Muffins, 114

Nut Butter (peanut butter substitute),
146
Nut Milk (milk substitute), 145

Oatmeal, 81
Oatmeal Bran Muffins, 152
Oatmeal Cookies, 117
Oatmeal Muffins, 114

Oatmeal Plus, 87
Oatmeal Sheet Cake, 154
Orange Fruit Punch, 142

Pancakes
Baked Apple Pancake, 119
Buckwheat Pancakes, 149
Cottage Cheese Pancakes, 97
Family Whole-wheat Pancakes, 120
Josh's Tofu Pancakes, 148
Potato Pancakes, 96
Rice Pancakes, 149
Rice Waffles, 150
Whole Wheat Pancakes, 96
Zucchini Pancakes, 96
Party Cubes, 116
Peanut Butter 'n Oatmeal Cookies, 117
Peanut Butter Bread, 113
Peanut Butter Carob Fudge, 153
Peanut Butter Delight, 101
Peanut Butter Deluxe Sandwich, 110
Peanut butter substitute, Nut Butter,
146
Peanut Butter-Tofu Deluxe, 148
Pita-Pinto Sandwich, 109
Potato Pancakes, 96
Potato Salad, 126
Potato Soup, 128
Potatoes Deluxe, 100
Pudding(s)
Baby Rice Pudding, 88
Elizabeth's Peanut Butter Pudding,
101

Rainy Day Play, Kid's Stuff, 118
Laura's Playdough, 118
Raisin and Bran Muffins, 114
Red, White, & Blue Special, 141
Rice 'n Beans, 91
Rice Cereal, 81
Rice Pancakes, 149
Rice Waffles, 150
Rice, Oat, or Barley Cereal, 82
Rice-Squash, 94
Rye Bread, 150

Salad Dressing(s)
Sesame Seed Salad Dressing, 124
Summer Salad Dressing, 126
Salad(s)
Carrot Salad, 99
Toddle Salad, 112
Antipasto Salad, 125
Apple Salad, 127
Fruit Salad, 127
Potato Salad, 126
Spinach Salad, 125
Sprouts Salad, 126
Taboulie, 124

Sandwiches
  Avocado & Cheese Sandwich, 121
  Cheese Muffin, 110
  Cheese Tortillas, 111
  Egg Salad Sandwich, 122
  Falafel Burgers, 137
  Greek Pita Sandwich, 121
  Lentil Cheeseburgers, 95
  Luncheon Bagels, 110
  Peanut Butter Deluxe Sandwich, 110
  Pita-Pinto Sandwich, 109
Sesame Seed Salad Dressing, 124
Simple Banana Smoothie, 86
Smoothies, 86
Snacks
  Fruit Leather, 144
  Tamari Nut Mix, 144
Soup(s)
  Carrot 'n Bean Soup, 91
  Cucumber Soup, 129
  Lentil Soup, 129
  Lentil Stew, 112
  Potato Soup, 128
Soy Milk (milk substitute), 145
Spaghetti Sauce, 132
Spaghetti Squash, 133
Special Day Cereal, 120
Special Day Sundae, 117
Spinach, how to steam, 139
Spinach Dip, 127
Spinach Lasagna, 133
Spinach Salad, 125
Spinach Sea Shells, 134
Spreads and Dips
  Chick Pea Delight, 122
  Chickie Dip, 111
  Cottage Cheese Delight, 111
  Guacamole, 128
  Honey Butter, 109
  Peanut Butter Delight, 101
  Peanut Butter-Tofu Deluxe, 148
  Spinach Dip, 127
  Tofu Dips, 147
  Tofu Mayonnaise, 147
Sprouts, how to grow, 98-99
Sprouts Salad, 126
Squash Milk (milk substitute), 145
Steamed Vegetables, 84
Stuffed Baked Zucchini, 139
Summer Salad Dressing, 126

Sunflower Bread, 123
Sunny Smoothie, 106

Taboulie, 124
Tamari Nut Mix, 144
Toddle Salad, 112
Tofu Dips, 147
Tofu Mayonnaise, 147
Tofu-Banana Whip, 87
Tropical Banana Sundae, 142

Vegetable Lunch, 99
Vegetable(s)
  Appled Sweet Potatoes, 101
  Baby Vegetable Purée, 84
  Baked Acorn Squash, 101
  Baked Sweet Potatoes, 100
  Broccoli & Rice, 91
  Broiled Zucchini, 138
  Cabbage, Zucchini & Tomato Bake,
    137
  Carrot-Zucchini Shred, 100
  Cheesy Creamy Spinach, 139
  Easy Scalloped Potatoes, 138
  Eggplant Parmesan, 134
  Garden Casserole, 95
  Potatoes Deluxe, 100
  Spaghetti Squash, 133
  Steamed Vegetables, 84
  Vegetable Lunch, 99
  Veggie Platter, 128
  Zucchini Cheese Bake, 138
Veggie Platter, 128

Whole-wheat Pancakes, 96
Whole-wheat Biscuits, 112
Whole-wheat Bread, 123
Wonderful Wheatberry Bread, 151

Yogurt, helpful tips for making, 85
Yogurt
  Bunny Yogurt, 100
  Bunny Yogurt, II, 100
  Homemade, 85
Yogurt Popsicles, 115

Zachary's Own Shake, 142
Zachary's Peanut Butter Balls, 141
Zucchini Cheese Bake, 138
Zucchini Pancakes, 96